10 Commandments of Personal Branding

By Erik Deckers and Robert Bagley

Foreword by Chonsten Jennings

10 Commandments of Personal Branding
By Erik Deckers and Robert Bagley
Foreword by Chonsten Jennings

Co-Pilot Publishing, Blountsville, AL 35031.

First Printing, 2025

Printed on acid-free paper

ISBN 13: 979-8-9908542-6-0

CO-PILOT PUBLISHING
Navigating Success Together

Co-Pilot Publishing, 2025

Foreword

Have you ever found yourself in a season where you didn't know what was next — or better yet, didn't even know who you were?

Yeah... I've been there.

I come from a background of working closely with high-level professionals and youth athletes in the basketball world. I've sat courtside, in boardrooms, and across from people who were considered somebody. I was often seen as someone of influence — I had the presence, the access, the relationships.

But if I'm being real, I didn't always feel influential.

Because influence without internal alignment isn't power — it's pressure.

I realized I was living out someone else's version of success. Maybe it was projected dreams from family. Maybe it was mentors I looked up to who meant well but didn't fully see me. Somewhere along the way, I became a mirror of other people's expectations... and in the process, I lost connection with who I truly was.

That was the turning point. Not the launch of a business, not a viral moment — but the choice to start rediscovering myself.

And that's when my personal brand began to grow. Not because I was trying to be branded, but because I was finally becoming aligned.

Looking back, I can clearly see the journey unfolded through three phases. Each one challenged me, grew me, and redefined what influence really meant.

Phase 1: Alignment and Fulfillment

This was the season I had to ask: What actually feels like mine?

What gives me peace? What makes me feel full, not just busy? I stopped choosing opportunities based on optics and started choosing alignment. That meant saying no to what no longer fit. It also meant trusting myself enough to create new lanes when none existed.

And in that alignment, I found energy. I found clarity. I found momentum that couldn't be manufactured — because it was mine.

Phase 2: Leading with Value

Once I was grounded in who I was, I had space to focus on what I could give.

I started paying attention to the rooms I entered — not to impress, but to impact. I asked better questions. I stopped trying to pitch and started listening more deeply. That's when I learned something I live by now: people don't remember your role — they remember your energy.

The way you leave people feeling is your real résumé. That's your brand.

Phase 3: Embodying My Future Self

Then came the discipline: Can I consistently show up as the future version of myself right now?

It's easy to talk about who we want to become. It's harder to act like them before the title, the platform, or the stage comes. I had to start honoring the future me with present-day decisions. That meant walking with more integrity, showing up on days I didn't feel like it, and choosing growth over comfort, repeatedly.

And that work paid off — not in followers or applause, but in peace. In purpose. In power that didn't need a spotlight to be real.

That journey ultimately birthed The Luminary Panel — a movement that became a mirror for others who, like me, were trying to find their lane.

At The Luminary Panel, we connect aspiring entrepreneurs to the stories and strategies of inspiring entrepreneurs — and more importantly, we become immediate resources. No gatekeeping. No fluff. Just real tools, real relationships, and real results.

I often say, when we're building something, we're really giving our younger selves the tools we needed — while handing those same tools to someone else on the rise. That's what makes the brand bigger than us.

And that's exactly what this book captures.

This isn't just a guide on how to look good online.

This is about how to live well offline.

It's about identity, intentionality, and impact.

It's about building something that speaks for you when you're not in the room.

So, as you read The 10 Commandments of Personal Branding, don't just skim the pages. Sit with them. Apply them. Live them. Let them serve as checkpoints in your own journey — not to become someone new, but to become more of who you really are.

Your future self is already watching.

Show up in a way they'd be proud of.

Before I close, I'd be remiss not to share this:

In the process of building my personal brand —
and launching what would eventually become The
Luminary Panel — I crossed paths with Robert
Bagley and Erik Deckers. Not only did their work
inspire me, but their example reminded me of
what it really means to live your brand out loud,
with service, clarity, and consistency. Our
conversations were never just informational —
they were transformational.

Connecting with them affirmed that I wasn't
alone in this work. It reminded me that building a
brand isn't about being seen — it's about
being useful. And if you let the principles in this
book take root in your life the way they did in
mine, your impact will multiply far beyond what
you can see right now.

—

Chonsten Jennings
Founder & CEO, The Luminary Panel

Introduction

The genesis of this mini-book began when Erik Deckers and I sat on a panel together at Z Co-Space and Clubhouse, a vibrant co-working and networking hub in The Mills/Ivanhoe District of Orlando – run and owned by Ayman Shamaa. This space fosters young entrepreneurs as they refine their craft and build exciting businesses.

One of those entrepreneurs, Chonsten Jennings, Founder and CEO of The Luminary Panel—a podcast that inspires people toward entrepreneurship and personal & professional growth—played a key role in bringing Erik and me together. Chonsten had invited both of us as guests in separate episodes during the first season of his podcast. Early in the season, I suggested to Chonsten that after Season One wrapped up, he should host a launch party featuring all the guest speakers as a panel. The goal was to invite the community to engage with these speakers on topics like networking, personal branding, ideation, business development, and professional growth.

The event was a resounding success. It was well-attended, and it ignited a chain of events that led to a monthly networking gathering at Z Co-Space. Out of this, a new coaching program for aspiring entrepreneurs emerged—The Purpose Engine.

The Season One Luminary Panel launch party took place in February 2024, coinciding with the release of my mini-book, *The 10 Commandments of Strategic Networking*. This book inspired me to approach Erik with the idea of co-authoring a sequel. As I learned more about Erik's writing career, I discovered that he had previously written about personal branding, including his 2017 co-authored book with Kyle Lacy, *Branding Yourself: How to Use Social Media to Invent or Reinvent Yourself* (available here).

At the same time, I had recently joined a publishing startup called Co-Pilot Books (www.copilotbooks.org), a platform designed to help aspiring authors get their books published. I took on the role of Chief Revenue Consultant and Author Coach. Among our first publishing wins was signing Emily Godwin, a new children's book author I met at Z Co-Space. She wrote and illustrated *Life To Me, Life To You* (available here). My own mini-book, *The 10 Commandments of Strategic Networking*, soon followed (available here).

Another major milestone was bringing in bestselling author Gary Wayne to produce the audiobooks for his two-part theological classic, The Genesis 6 Conspiracy. With hundreds of thousands of downloads in Kindle and paperback, his works are now thriving in audiobook format, ranking #1 in their categories on Audible, iTunes, and Amazon (available here & here).

Back to my collaboration with Erik—once we decided to write this book together, we developed a rhythm for crafting each chapter. We would meet in person, hashing out ideas on one of the "10 Commandments of Personal Branding." Erik would then take our discussions, write the respective chapter, and send me a draft for review.

This process set in motion a fifteen-month writing cadence, where Erik and I met every four to six weeks over pizza at Lazy Moon Pizza (www.lazymoonpizza.com) on University Blvd in Orlando (Erik's favorite pizza place in Central Florida.) The eclectic atmosphere, artistic décor, and vintage photos made it the perfect space for creativity. Each session lasted about 90 minutes, with Erik recording our conversation while we brainstormed the content. He then transformed the recordings into chapters using his extraordinary writing style—one that I'm confident you'll enjoy in this book.

Robert Bagley

About the Authors

Erik Deckers

Erik Deckers is a seasoned writer, speaker, and humorist who has been crafting words professionally for over 30 years. He has been a newspaper humor columnist since 1994 and has been blogging since 1997.

Erik is also the president of Pro Blog Service, a content marketing agency that helps businesses enhance their online presence, and he's the co-author of several books on social media and personal branding, including *Branding Yourself: How to Use Social Media to Invent or Reinvent Yourself*, *No Bullshit Social Media*, and *The Owned Media Doctrine*.

He's also a sought-after speaker who has delivered presentations on topics like personal branding, content marketing, and the effective use of humor in the workplace. His engaging speaking style combines informative content with a touch of stand-up comedy flair.

Finally, Erik served as the Spring 2016 writer-in-residence at the Jack Kerouac House in Orlando, Florida, and currently holds the position of president of the Kerouac Project. He resides in Orlando, where he continues to write, speak, and share his unique blend of humor and insight with audiences nationwide.

Robert Bagley

Robert is a dynamic and award-winning executive leader with a proven track record of driving personal and professional growth across industries. A true catalyst for transformation, he has helped public and private enterprises achieve extraordinary success by building high-performance sales teams, fostering cohesive cultures, and steering organizations toward their highest potential. His leadership is defined by trust, professionalism, and unwavering integrity—on and off the job.

Throughout his career, Robert has consistently surpassed revenue and profitability goals while ensuring organizations deliver best-in-class service. His ability to elevate customer satisfaction, optimize business operations, and enhance stakeholder value has made him a sought-after strategist in corporate growth and leadership development. He excels in designing and executing innovative processes, programs, and strategies that drive sustainable success.

His experience spans business engagements and leadership training in Israel, Germany, Mexico, and Canada, deepening his insights into diverse markets and cultures. Robert firmly believes in the power of cross-organizational teamwork, technology-driven solutions, and strategic problem-solving—elements that have repeatedly fueled revenue growth and strengthened lasting business partnerships.

Now, Robert shares his expertise as a business, sales, and career coach, empowering entrepreneurs, executives, and professionals to harness the power of their personal brand. Through his guidance, individuals can unlock their unique strengths, maximize career opportunities, and achieve lasting business success.

Chapter 1
What Is Your Personal Brand?

If you're in the business world or are about to enter it, you need to think about your personal brand. That is, how do people think about you in your relationship with them?

How do they think about you in the context of your relationship? How do they think you will perform in a certain situation or on a certain project?

Your personal brand is basically the emotional response that people have about you when you're not around.

It's the "Oh, good!" and "Oh, s#!t!" response.

Everyone you meet thinks those two things about you, once when you're coming and once when you're going. *When* they say those things depends totally on you.

That's your personal brand.

Ideally, you want them to say "Oh, good!" when you arrive and "Oh, s#!t!" when you leave, but not everyone gets that response. For some people, it's the complete opposite. You probably know a few of those people yourself.

This book is dedicated to helping you build your personal brand in the business world, helping you get the "Oh, good!" when you show up. To getting people to think positively about you when you're not around. To becoming the kind of person others recommend when they need help with a particular problem or are looking for capable people to work on a project.

To become a positive personal brand, you've got to be relentlessly focused on what you do that adds value to other people's lives, as well as your own. But all of that starts when you know what you want your personal brand to be.

Start by Defining Your Personal Brand

You need to define your personal brand early on because this is the framework that you are going to build your future on. It's going to set up your future actions and behaviors and may even dictate some of the decisions you make. Here's how to start defining your personal brand.

1. Reflect on Your Identity. Who are you at your core? What are your values, strengths, and passions? Your personal brand should reflect your authentic self, so reflect on the things you like doing. Rather than just stating, "I'm going to be good at X," figure out what you're already good at instead. There's no point in reinventing the wheel when you're already riding a perfectly good bicycle. Pick the thing you can do and enjoy doing, because your ultimate goal is to find a way to make money at it.

Both Robert and Erik were able to figure this out early on after they reflected on the things they enjoyed doing and talking to people about.

Robert knew, based on his work in sales and networking, that he liked solving problems — an ideal skill for someone in sales. Whenever someone had a problem, he loved having the solution that could solve the problem for them. He could solve problems for sales prospects, and he could introduce someone from his network to that person as a way to help them out.

Erik loved writing, and he loved teaching. And he found that he could teach people important information through writing. He was able to turn his love of writing into a way to help move him along in his career, taking jobs where writing was critical, until he became the owner of a content marketing agency.

And we both love connecting people. We strive to be connectors, putting people together so they can help each other, learn from each other, and make improvements to their own lives and situations.

According to Malcolm Gladwell's book, *The Tipping Point*, connectors are people specialists and they link us up with the world. They know and maintain contact with many people, and they tend to associate with other connectors, so they have a rich and extensive network of friends, associates, and referrals.

So we have both made it a point to connect people with other people as a part of our brand, and it has served us well.

2. Define Your Unique Value Proposition.

Once you know what you want to be known for, now you need to figure out what makes you stand out from the crowd. What value do you bring to the table that others do not?

In business, your Unique Value Proposition (also called the Unique Selling Proposition) is that one thing that sets you apart from everyone else. If you have a product or service, what does it do that your competition doesn't do?

For example, a personal finance app's USP would say, "Financial Serenity understands your life, offers personalized insights and proactive guidance for your unique goals. Its AI-based "Future Forecast" tool warns you when your spending habits threaten to derail your goals through the use of a mild electric shock."

Having a USP is important if you're ever starting a business, but it's also important when you're applying for a job, working as a freelancer, or even dating. Knowing it will help keep you on track to pursue the goals, meet the people, and attend the events that will help build your brand. Without the mild electric shocks.

Your unique value proposition is your combination of skills, experiences, and qualities that make you valuable and attractive to others. Whether it's your creativity, problem-solving abilities, exceptional communication skills, or your extensive contact database, identify the qualities that set you apart and make that a central part of your personal brand.

3. Consider Other People's Perceptions.
Remember, your personal brand isn't about how you see yourself, it's about how others see you. That means if you want to be known for a certain thing, you had better make sure other people know that about you as well. There's no point in building your skills and brand in secret. If no one knows about it, do you really have a brand in the first place?

That means, if you really want to know what people think about you, ask them. Ask the people around you — teachers, friends, co-workers, bosses, and mentors — what words or traits they associate with you when you're not around. Talk to the people who care about you and want the best for you, because they'll give you good feedback.

But maybe not the people who will sugarcoat everything and tell you that everything you do is wonderful.

(Thanks, Mom!)

I mean, we love our parents, but they're not going to give you the honest feedback that you actually need, except that maybe you don't call often enough.

It's going to be tough to do because the conversations can be rather awkward, but the feedback you get can help you shape your personal brand effectively.

On the other hand, you don't have to make all the changes everyone tells you about because they don't know you or the people you're trying to interact with.

Just be aware that there's an element of truth in everything people tell you. It's not always completely true, but if more than a few people mention it, you should at least consider that they're seeing something you're not. And you may have one person who is completely off the mark, so feel free to ignore them. But pay attention if several people are all off the mark about the same thing — they may see something you don't.

So, carefully consider the feedback you receive and decide which aspects you want to act on. Not all feedback will be relevant or applicable to you, so pick and choose the information you want to take to heart and which ones you want to ignore.

Use AI to help you

We're not above using artificial intelligence in our work. After all, it's a great analyst and it can see things that we're missing. So, if you have been using a generative AI for any length of time — ChatGPT, Gemini, Perplexity, or Claude — work with that one, because it has the ability to assess you already. Give it this prompt:

```
You're a personal branding
consultant. I want a thorough
analysis of my personal brand.
Please review my LinkedIn
profile [URL], my blog/website
[URL], and my social media
channels [URLs].

In your response, I want you to:
```

- Define my current personal brand by summarizing my voice, strengths, and unique qualities.
- Identify my brand pillars: What are the core themes or values that come through in my work?
- Describe my target audience. Who should I speak to? Who is likely to engage with my content?
- Highlight my differentiators. What makes me stand out from others in my field?
- Suggest areas for improvement. Are there inconsistencies, missed opportunities, or ways to strengthen my brand?
- Recommend actionable next steps. How can I further develop or promote my personal brand?
- Offer a brand statement or tagline, like a Unique Value Proposition; something to use in bios or introductions.
- If you see any gaps in my online presence, tell me what I'm missing or what I

```
could add to support my
brand.
```

Be sure to bookmark that conversation (or pin it, if your AI has that capability; ChatGPT doesn't), and return to it occasionally. Tell it to look at new branding efforts, your updated LinkedIn profile, and new social networks. Ask it to reassess your brand every six months, and then ask it if it has noticed any changes.

You can also ask it to recommend blog articles that you should be writing, but *DO NOT USE AI TO WRITE THOSE ARTICLES FOR YOU.* It's morally dishonest, and it takes away the chance for you to develop your own voice. This is important if you want to become a thought leader. Try this prompt to come up with a few ideas:

```
Based on what you know about me,
what are 10 blog article ideas I
could write for my blog that
would establish me as a thought
leader?
```

4. Align Your Actions With Your Brand. Your brand is more than just what you say, it's what you do. That's the reputation that you leave with people, and it's what makes people say "Oh, good/oh, s#!t."

Make sure your actions align with the image you want to project. That includes your behavior in professional settings, your interactions with others, and the content you share on social media. It can even be your wardrobe and sense of style.

Consistency between your words and actions is critical to building that strong personal brand. Make sure your identity and unique value proposition align with your actions, and that will have a positive effect on people's perceptions about you.

Think of it this way: When novelists write a story or screenwriters write a script, they focus on the parts of their story that only drive the story forward. If it doesn't move the story, they cut it out completely. It may be a nice little scene where two characters get to discuss their dreams and profess their love for one another, but if it has nothing to do with the plot or the story, they cut it.

You need to take the same approach with the things that you do. The projects you take on, the events you attend, and the groups you join, you have to consider whether they drive your brand forward. That's what it means to make sure your actions align with your brand.

If they don't drive your story forward, cut them out. Focus only on the things that actually contribute to your brand and give you the opportunity to add to it.

That's not to say you have to cut out all the fun stuff in your life, so you only focus on your brand. But if you're trying to build your own business, it doesn't make sense to start another one at the same time. If you want to start your own marketing agency, that's not the time to start studying for your real estate license. If you want to be a realtor, be a realtor. But if you want to own a marketing agency, then that should be your focus. The real estate license doesn't drive your story forward, and it doesn't align with your personal brand.

5. Consider Your Legacy. Think about the lasting impact you want to have on the world. What do you want to be remembered for? Your legacy is just the long-term result of aligning your actions with your brand.

Remember, your personal brand is what people think about you when you're not in the room. Your legacy is what people remember about you long after you've died. (Sorry for the morbid thought, but that's exactly what legacy is: personal branding for dead people.)

For some of you, your legacy may be decades in the future. (Fingers crossed.) For others, it's not that far off. But no matter where it is in your future, thoughts of legacy need to influence what you do in your work and relationships: The actions you take today will have long-lasting effects on your future and how people remember you after you're gone.

While your personal brand can open up new opportunities for you (or close them off), your life's journey is all a part of your legacy, and you will make and create memories for others along the way.

Let's say you make a mid-career shift, switching from one field to a completely different one. Your previous life is part of your legacy; the future you create is part of your legacy. The things you do for others, the time you spend with your family, the friends you make, the coworkers you support — all of that contributes to your legacy.

Whether you want to make a difference in your community, leave a mark in your industry, or inspire others, defining your legacy can provide clarity to your personal brand building.

6. Set Goals for Your Brand. You decide to go on a road trip with a friend. You get the snacks, you prepare a couple playlists (in our day, you'd make mix tapes), and you gas up the car. You pull out of the driveway and. . . where are you even going? You didn't pick a destination, so you have no idea which direction to drive, which route to take.

Even a vague idea — "let's go to Oregon" — is certainly better than "I don't know, just drive, man." At least you have some idea of which direction to start driving.

That's how it is with personal branding. In order to *build* your brand, you have to know where you want your personal brand to *go*. You need a destination so you can start driving in that direction. But it's better to actually have specific, measurable goals in life, so you can actually know if you're meeting them or not.

"Speak in public more" is not that measurable. What is more? Did you speak at all last year? If not, then one gig qualifies as more. So does five, ten, and one presentation every week.

A better goal is "Speak in public 12 times in one year, averaging one speech per month." That's easy, measurable, and it gives you a deadline. You know immediately after one month whether you're meeting your average. You know at the end of the year whether you succeeded at that goal.

7. Roll with the changes. Your goals absolutely will change in your life as your life changes. Your destination for your road trip will change.

Sometimes you don't know what that is until the next season of your life starts and the next opportunity arises.

You're driving along on your road trip to Oregon, and halfway through, you say, "You know what? I'd rather go to Chicago!" Or there's a big blizzard ahead, which makes passing through the Upper Midwest impossible, so you decide to go to St. Louis instead. Or you become disillusioned with Oregon and decide to move to Florida instead.

Whatever that may be, your personal brand needs to evolve to rise to that occasion as well.

If you have been in the corporate world for a lot of years, and you decide you want to be a corporate speaker, you can't just declare yourself a speaker and wait for all the invitations to roll in.

You need to evolve to become a speaker. It means learning how to speak in public (attend Toastmasters or hire a speaking coach), becoming a thought leader (start a blog or write a book), and taking baby steps by giving free and cheap speeches in your local organizations (Chamber of Commerce, fraternal organizations). It means making new, specific, measurable goals and then changing your personal branding strategies to reach them. You chose a new destination on your road trip, and now you need to adjust your route to get there.

As you grow in your speaking skills and reputation, you can seek new paid speaking opportunities that take you to bigger stages and audiences. It will take a while, but you can get there. It just means setting goals and then taking the steps to get there, just like you've been doing all this time in your career.

Remember, personal branding isn't static; it should adapt to changes in your life circumstances and aspirations. And you need to adapt as well.

Live Your Brand PUBLICLY

We alluded to this earlier when we talked about aligning your actions with your brand, but that's more about just being a kind and helpful person. About living up to the positive perceptions that people have of you. About being authentic and transparent in who you are, and not putting on an act as part of your brand.

In living your brand, we mean actually doing the thing that you want to be known for. If you want to be known as a connector, then you need to attend networking events, meet a lot of people, and connect them to each other.

If you want to be a writer, that means not only writing but publishing and promoting your work. It means letting your writing be visible by sharing it on your blog, magazines, trade journals, or books. And then promoting it on social media. It also means joining writing groups, reading at open mic events, and attending writing conferences.

If you want to be known as an expert in your particular field, it means not only studying but sharing your expertise with others. Again, publish your ideas on your blog, guest post on other blogs, submit articles to industry trade journals, and give talks at conferences and special events. It also means promoting your ideas on social media and sharing them as often as you can.

In all these cases, you want people to see you living your brand without blatantly flogging your brand.

Personal branding doesn't mean wearing a t-shirt that says, "Customer service expert." It means actually practicing good customer service yourself. It means writing blog and journal articles about customer service. It means sharing examples of great customer service that you experienced and writing case studies of companies that practice good customer service. And it means speaking at a variety of conferences about how to do good customer service. (Also, get an embroidered polo shirt instead of a t-shirt; it's less tacky and more acceptable in business settings.)

It's one thing to focus on improving your skills, but promotion is equally important. You don't want to be the best-kept secret in your community or your industry. There's no point in being the smartest person in your chosen field if no one is there to 1) see it or 2) hire you for it.

So, share your learning and experience journey on social media. Publish your work in public settings.

Even if there are only 20 people who see it, that's 20 people who know you're very good at what you do. Those 20 people might be decision makers, or are connected to decision makers, and that could lead to new opportunities for you.

But you have to share it all in the first place.

Protect Your Brand

Building your brand takes commitment and consistency, but it's more than just getting things done or doing good deeds. It's about fulfilling promises, upholding values, and most importantly, avoiding actions that could harm your brand.

Protecting your brand means making sure others think highly of you, even when you're not around. That means treating them with kindness, respect, and consideration. It means valuing their time and their feelings.

It also means protecting yourself by the actions you take or how you let others see you.

Ever since the early days of social media, Erik made it a personal policy to never let people take a photo of him with an alcoholic drink in his hand. Not because he's opposed to alcohol, but because it could raise a lot of questions in other people's minds.

"Does he drink a lot? Does he party frequently? Does he make smart choices about his drinking? What if he doesn't? How does that translate into his business decisions?"

It's unlikely that a single photo of Erik with a beer in his hand is going to smash his reputation, but it's easier to make a commitment to an absolute rule for yourself than trying to decide which photos are going to be harmful and which ones aren't. You constantly have to decide, "Should I follow it this time or protect myself?"

It's like Mark Twain once said, "If you tell the truth, you don't have to remember anything." Similarly, if Erik commits to never having a photo taken of him with a drink in his hand, he never has to decide whether it's OK or not for each photo.

Failure to maintain your personal standards can erode your hard-earned reputation. A single misstep or breach of trust can undo years of dedicated effort and damage your credibility irreparably.

Remember, *a reputation takes years to build and seconds to destroy.*

You've no doubt seen or at least heard about Will Smith slapping Chris Rock at the 2022 Oscars after Rock made a joke about Jada Pinkett Smith, Will Smith's wife.

The public backlash was immediate, the fallout began, and Smith faced a huge blow to his own reputation. Netflix canceled a series sequel to his urban fantasy action film, *Bright;* he resigned from the Academy of Motion Picture Arts and Sciences, and they banned him for ten years; and his film, *Emancipation*, was delayed partly due to the negative publicity surrounding The Slap.

It reminds us of an old joke:

Two guys were sitting on top of a hill that overlooked their small town, just shooting the breeze. At one point, one of the guys sighs deeply as he looks down at his town, and the friend asks what's wrong.

"Look at that town down there," said the first guy. "You see the bridge crossing the river that leads into our town? I built that bridge with my own two hands. But do they call me Edward the Bridge Builder? No."

"And do you see the Church overlooking the square? I built that Church with my own two hands. And do they call me Edward the Church Builder? No."

He pauses for a moment and says, "But kiss ONE sheep."

No matter what Smith does with the rest of his life, this is what people will remember first and foremost. He's at least wealthy enough that it doesn't matter if he never works again.

Ultimately, brand protection isn't just about avoiding negativity; it's about actively cultivating a positive reputation based on trust, reliability, and authenticity.

Chapter 2 Discovering Your Value

Building your personal brand means finding your own value. Not your net worth, the value you give to others, or even the value of your own body. (**Fun fact:** The elements in the human body are worth about $585.)

Rather, your value is a hidden treasure that's inside you. It's made up of your passion and skills: the things you love to do and are good at. When you know what you love and what you're good at, you understand your value. When you know that, you bring something special to every relationship.

For example, Erik is passionate about writing and good at public speaking. So he loves teaching other people how to improve their writing, giving seminars, speaking at conferences, or offering training sessions at corporations. Robert is passionate about networking and good at selling. So he loves meeting new potential customers by introducing people to each other, attending networking events, and joining different networking organizations in his community. (See Chapter 4, The Importance of Networking.)

Finding your value helps you connect with other people, both in business and in life. People appreciate it when you bring something valuable to the table, and they're more likely to help you in return, which creates a vast network of support and opportunities that get shared throughout the network you have built. That can be as simple as introducing you to someone who needs your help, or even helping you find an opportunity to express your value.

To be able to do all that, you first need to find and define your value.

How Do You Find Your Value?

It all starts with finding your passions. Finding the stuff you love to do, the stuff that — if it were possible — you would do for a living, doing nothing but that particular thing.

Maybe it's writing or speaking in public. It's selling and meeting new people. Or it's creating the perfect Excel sheet. Or you love spring cleaning and organizing. Or woodworking. Or restoring an old car. Or it's something as simple as taking care of animals and taking them on walks.

You wouldn't believe the number of people who don't even know what their passion is. They don't know what it is they love to do. They go to work at a job they probably hate, doing things that leave them unfulfilled. They come home, turn on the TV, and don't move until it's time for bed. Then they get up in the morning and do it all over again.

They may have something they like doing on the weekends — a hobby, a fandom, a passing interest. But they don't love what they do, and they have no idea how they would even go about figuring that out. They don't have any goals or plans for their future because they don't know what they even *want* to do five or ten years from now.

What's worse is they may truly love their weekend hobby, but they don't think of it as their passion; it's not something they would ever think about pursuing. It's just something to look forward to throughout the week, but it's not their focus in life.

When we say "find your passion," we mean find the thing at work that you love to do. Maybe — and this may sound weird — you love making Excel spreadsheets. Maybe you love selling. Maybe you love working in renewable energy.

We don't necessarily mean "turn your hobby into your job." But we do mean find the thing that you love to do at work and want to do more of. Find the thing you actually love doing and would like to do more of. Find the thing you want to learn more about, read about, listen to podcasts about, and become an expert at.

For Robert, it was networking and selling. He found he loved it, so he devoted his entire professional life to getting better at selling than he was the year before. He listened (and still listens) to audiobooks on selling. He listens to podcasts and interviews with excellent salespeople. And he works to improve his skills at getting people to buy from him.

As a result, the *value* that he brings to his employer is being able to sell their product to as many customers as he can. He takes the thing he loves — selling — and applies that to his employer's products. He could change companies or industries, and his passion and skills would go with him.

Whether he's selling flooring, commercial office furniture, building supplies, office equipment, or chainsaws, when Robert is selling, he's in his element, bringing his value to his employer.

Once you find your passion, you'll find your value. Because not everyone loves the thing you do. Not everyone is as good as that thing as you are.

Not everyone loves to sell. Not everyone loves to design websites. Not everyone loves to write. They don't have the skills, time, or energy to get that kind of work done, and they don't want to figure out how to do it. They don't want to spend years doing something they don't enjoy just so they can be mediocre at it.

This is where you come in. This is where you can step up, hands on your hips in a classic superhero pose, and boldly declare, "There's no need to fear! *I* am here!" (If you actually do this, please let us know because we want to hear how that went. And send us a photo.)

For example, Erik is a professional writer who owns his own copywriting agency. He ghostwrites blog articles for corporations and books for people. Why? Because not everyone wants to write blog articles or a book. They don't know how, they can't put the time into it every week, and they don't want to take the years needed to be good at it.

He was fortunate to find a thing he loved to do *and* was good at, and could then provide value to other people by writing for them. He was able to turn that passion into an entire career. He may not spend his time writing satirical humor novels or TV sitcoms, which is his first love. But he's been able to turn his personal passion into a career.

By finding your passion, you can find your value and offer something that no one else can to a potential employer or a customer.

Sometimes, "Pursue Your Passion" Is Dumb Advice

"Do what you love, and you'll never work a day in your life."

Have you heard this before? It sounds great. What if you could earn a nice, fat salary by doing the thing you love the most — your favorite hobby or activity? Wouldn't that be great if you could make a living being a professional accordion player, a model builder, or a poet?

Except we're going to contradict ourselves here. We just told you to pursue your passion, find the thing you love to do, and figure out a way to make money at it. But there are times when this is a really bad idea. Like really, terribly bad. Because there are times when trying to make a living out of your passion is just not a good idea.

You have to look at the commercial value of your interest and figure out if 1) you *can* make a living at it, and 2) you want to spend 40 – 60 hours a week doing it.

For example, let's say you love to knit. Any time you've got free time, you've got a pair of knitting needles in your hand and you're producing a sweater every two weeks. You've even got those professional needle sets, which is just two needles joined by a heavy-gauge wire like a pair of knitting nunchucks. You think to yourself, "Wouldn't it be great if I could just knit sweaters for my job?"

It would be nice, but it's not possible or feasible.

Let's imagine (for nice round numbers) that you need to make $72,000 to make a comfortable living. Ignoring all the business logistics and details for the moment, you need to generate $6,000 per month or $1500 per week.

If you normally produce one sweater every two weeks, you have to sell each sweater for $3,000 to earn your $6,000. Good luck with that. If you can find 24 people to buy $3,000 sweaters, you can pull it off, except the most expensive sweaters we found online were $1,400, so that's out.

More likely, you'll have to price your sweaters at $100 apiece and sell 60 of them every month, which means you have to produce 15 sweaters per week — that's three per day if you want your weekends free, or 2.14 sweaters per day if you work every day.

Does that even sound possible? Even if it is, it's probably exhausting. You'll have to work at top speed *all the time* to meet that demand. No breaks, no days off, no slowing down.

Now your favorite hobby of knitting has become a job, and you'll grow to hate it even more than the worst job you ever had. You'll look for a new hobby instead, like working in a hot restaurant kitchen during the dinner rush, or cramming yourself into a tiny cubicle to answer angry phone calls just to get some relief from knitting 2.14 sweaters per day.

Be "Passion Adjacent"

So, how do you follow your passion and make money at it when we just told you that's a dumb idea? You already know you're not going to make a living knitting sweaters (or playing guitar or playing video games), but you want your passion to align with your work. You want to make your passion a part of your income stream, but it's not economically feasible. What then?

The best way is to work *near* that field, but not actually do it.

If you love knitting, maybe you can work for a hobby store or fabric store. If you love playing music, go into sales at a music store or become a sales rep for a music manufacturer. If you like playing video games, work for a video game company or a video game news outlet.

This way, you get to work near your field, immersing yourself in the thing you love, but not actually spending your time doing that thing 8 – 10 hours per day.

Rather than making a living doing your hobby, you can make a living by supporting it.

The Difference Between Skills and Passions

So if you can't do the work that your passion brings, what about the work that you're good at? What if you could devote your career to doing the things you excel at and do better than most people? Not things like playing video games, writing, or knitting. But the administrative skills, the tech skills, or just the things that no one else likes to do.

Admittedly, it's not as sexy as, say, playing guitar in front of thousands of screaming fans or writing a best-selling novel. But these are still skills that you can bring to the table.

For example, Robert is really good at tracking expenses and bookkeeping. He has to do it for work, but he also does it for his own family. He helps his daughter with her business — she's a professional influencer — and he does all the bookkeeping for her business; he also does the books for his publishing company; and he just completed a very lengthy expense report that covered the last two months for his current employer.

He doesn't love it; it's not his passion. He doesn't put on a costume and solve bookkeeping crimes at night, although that would be pretty cool.

(Seriously, can you imagine? "Step aside, folks! The Abacus is here!")

But it's something that he's able to do for his employer and his family, and because he's good at it, he can at least get some enjoyment out of it while he does it. He may not be passionate about it, but he likes it, and sometimes, that's good enough.

This is important because sometimes doing the thing you're good at can lead to your passion. Let's say you have spent your entire career working in operations for a manufacturer. You like the process, you like figuring out problems, and you like making sure the operation runs efficiently and on time.

So the next stage of your career doesn't have to be at another manufacturing operation. You could be an operations consultant, helping other manufacturers find their own efficiencies and improvements. You're doing the thing you like and are good at, and you're getting paid for it!

Being able to do bookkeeping lets Robert do the things he *is* passionate about: selling, running a publishing company, and helping his family follow their passions.

Once you discover your value, it's time to find ways to bring that to your relationships.

Chapter 3
What Value Can You Bring to a Relationship?

Creating value in your relationships is the foundation of success in both your personal and professional networks. It's not the number of people in your Rolodex,[1] it's not the number of people in your LinkedIn Connections. And it's certainly never the number of cards you give away at networking events or the number of cards you collect. (Don't even get us started on those guys.)

You could have 3,000 connections on LinkedIn, but if you've never met a single one of them in person, you're not going to provide very much value.

For example, it's an acceptable practice to ask a LinkedIn connection for an introduction to someone else in a person's network. You could

---

[1] For all you under-30 readers, a Rolodex is a 20th-century version of your phone list written out on small cards and stored on a cylindrical device that you spin around to find the card you want.

email someone and say, "I see you're connected to Bert O'Higgins on LinkedIn. Could you introduce me to him?"

Imagine how frustrating it is when that person says, "Oh, I don't actually know Bert O'Higgins. I'm connected to over 20,000 people, but I've certainly never interacted with him."

How valuable is that person's network, then? What kind of value is your friend bringing to their relationship with Bert, let alone with you? Are they even a good networker if more than 95% of their social network is just anonymous people halfway around the world that they've never even met face-to-face?

That's probably the last time you'll ask that person for help because they've just shown you that their network is pretty valueless.

Whether you're in business, a creative endeavor, or just making everyday connections, bringing value to others is the key to building trust, collaborating, and creating long-lasting partnerships. The process is about more than just swapping business cards or even just exchanging services or favors. It's about building relationships with people you can actually help because you've actually met them and know who they are.

It's certainly not a question of going to a networking event and handing out as many cards as you can, like a Vegas blackjack dealer. (Don't be like those people. You don't count success by the number of cards you gave away. There's a very good chance that most of those cards ended up in the trash.)

We can't tell you the number of people we've met at networking events who just hold a stack of business cards in their hands like they're about to deal out a magic trick. They approach a small knot of people, introduce themselves, whip out their cards, and then walk away. Oftentimes, they don't even stick around to learn who you are. They just think, "Welp, I connected with those people. Now to wait for the calls to come rolling in!"

Erik has seen people like this at two consecutive networking meetings, but they never come to a third. They probably assume it's a low-value group and save their energy for pestering someone else.

Bringing value to a relationship is about understanding what the other person needs and offering to help them with no expectations of an immediate payoff. It's about creating a meaningful relationship that benefits both parties in the long term.

The heart of this approach is the idea of giving first, offering value without an agenda, and knowing that it will come back to you in unexpected and beneficial ways.

This mindset is called "Givers Gain," and it highlights how giving selflessly creates a cycle of reciprocity, where new opportunities and success will naturally follow. (We'll talk more about it in a minute.)

The art of bringing value to relationships is not just about financial exchanges that benefit you. It's not about doing favors for someone so they'll do favors for you. It's not about getting someone to "owe you one."

Instead, it involves insights, connections, and the willingness to help others achieve their goals *first*.

Let's say that again so you don't miss it.

It's about being the *first* to be willing to be the *first* to help others achieve their goals *first*.

Did we mention you have to do it *first?*

(We'll talk more about this in a bit.)

By asking the right questions, becoming a trusted resource, and showing genuine interest in others, you'll become the kind of person that other people want to work with and be around.

So, let's look at how perception shapes relationships, how to offer meaningful value, and why focusing on relationships will lead to greater opportunities for everyone involved.

Perception: The Person You Hope to Build Your Value With

In any networking situation, the key to adding value begins with understanding the person you want to connect with. If you want to build a relationship where you offer value, then you need to put yourself in the shoes of the person you're engaging with.

Perception is important in this process, not just about how you see yourself, but how the other person sees you.

Business professionals — and that includes creative professionals like filmmakers, writers, and graphic designers — all face the same challenge: breaking through from being a perceived outsider to being someone who brings value to the relationship. How you're perceived by others will ultimately determine how much influence you have and how much the other person will be willing to receive from you.

For example, Robert has received unsolicited auditions for some of his film scripts, which is a sign that his work is already being perceived as something valuable enough for people to send their work without being asked. This is the power of creating a favorable, valuable impression: It attracts people to you.

This perception is not built on just one interaction, like handing someone your card at a networking event. It's shaped over time and in future interactions — how you act, how you follow up, how you show your reliability, and how you contribute without expecting anything in return.

All of these elements define how others see you.

People tend to remember whether you offer value without a hidden agenda. If you can do that, you build trust through these consistent and thoughtful actions — this shapes the perception others have of you as a value-bringer.

What's interesting is that *you* don't always know what your value is until you've demonstrated it repeatedly by doing things that meet the other person's goals and desires. As you start pursuing the networking opportunities that resonate with you and making the offers that you're capable of delivering, then you'll get an idea that "Oh, maybe I *do* bring value to people."

How Do I Bring Value to Someone Else? How Do I Bring It to Me?

Understanding how you bring value gets to the heart of what it means to be a reliable and trusted partner in any relationship.

The answer begins with listening.

Bringing value is not just about what you can offer or what you can do for someone. It's about understanding what the other person needs. That starts with listening.

(**Note:** This is also the key to successful sales. Don't tell a potential customer all the cool stuff your product or service does. *Ask them what they need.* Then listen to the answer and show how you can solve their problems.)

Whether you help someone find a new customer, connect them with an important contact, or offer insights that can improve their business, bringing value means you are tuned into the goals and struggles of the person you're talking with.

One question Robert likes to ask people he's meeting with for the first time, especially his potential customers: "Who is a good customer for you?"

This opens the door for him to understand how he can assist others in a meaningful way. He might not know right away how he can help, but by asking direct and thoughtful questions like this, he can demonstrate that his focus is on their success, not his.

The more you help someone else this way, the more opportunities will naturally arise for them to help you in return, even if it's not readily apparent how.

Similarly, bringing value to yourself isn't about getting someone to "owe you one." Doing a favor for someone so they'll do a favor for you is a sad and lonely way to go through life. If you keep track of the favors people owe you, you will absolutely develop a reputation as someone who counts favors.

People won't want to work with you or help you. If you're a favor counter, people will absolutely do the one they owe you.

And then they'll never do another one for you again.

Instead, your goal should be to create a relationship where your reliability, consistency, and ability to offer valuable insights puts you in a position where others are eager to offer you opportunities.

Robert is a power LinkedIn user, and his network is large because he interacts with those people and builds online relationships with them. (He also meets a lot of people in real life and adds them to his online life.) He provides value by interacting with LinkedIn posts and replying to comments. This has helped build his reputation as someone who offers great insights.

He didn't expect people to just engage with his content, though; he actively sought to add value to their experience, whether it was through his comments, networking connections, or just being responsive.

Over time, these small actions built up and created a rich and vibrant network that sees him as a person of value.

The best way to add value on social media is to offer great information. Share interesting articles in your own industry, or share articles that will be interesting to different people in your network. Post the article and tag them so they see it.

Better yet, email them the link with a quick message: "I read this and thought of you." That little act tells the other person you're regularly thinking about how you can help them.

Givers Gain — You Reap What You Sow

The concept of Givers Gain comes to us through Business Networking International (BNI) and the book of the same name by Dr. Ivan Misner, founder of BNI, and Jeff Morris.

Givers Gain is fundamental to building long-term, mutually beneficial relationships. And it comes down to a simple truth: **you reap what you sow**.

In other words, helping others without expecting an immediate reward will eventually come back to you. Whether you call it a blessing or karma or cool points, if you do enough for other people — if you give — then you will gain.

When your goal is to help others and add value, people begin to see you as someone they can rely on. You'll build your reputation as a problem solver, a connector, and, ultimately, a leader.

Robert once met the president of a large janitorial company at a networking event. He didn't ask for anything upfront, but he talked to the president and listened to some of his concerns.

One thing the president struggled with was finding enough people to fill the open positions he had, so they could meet all of their customer obligations.

Robert connected him with a staffing agency that specialized in the janitorial services industry. By doing so, Robert created value by helping to solve a problem, even though there was no direct benefit to him at that time. Again, he didn't ask for anything; he just nurtured the relationship and continued to be helpful to not only the janitorial service *and* the staffing agency.

But over time, his efforts opened up new doors for him, both with the janitorial company and the staffing agency, because he had made himself indispensable to them both. He provided value for them and never asked for anything in return.

But it certainly came back to him. Both parties made new introductions to Robert that turned into business and sales for everyone. The staffing company also ended up placing several folks for Robert's employer at the time.

By acting as a Giver, you show that your focus is not purely transactional.

Instead, you're investing in a relationship that can eventually return the favor, often in ways you could never anticipate.

And it doesn't even come back directly to you. The person you help may return the favor one day, or they may mention your name to someone else, and that person mentions your name to a third person, and that person contacts you for help.

Let's say you own an IT consulting company, specializing in disaster prevention and recovering. One of your clients is a very small manufacturer with only two other employees and a small production facility in a tiny industrial park outside of town. Walter says he's having trouble keeping his finances in order and is having trouble finding efficiencies so he can grow.

So you introduce your bookkeeper, Jasmine, to Walter. Jasmine is good at her job, and she's able to help Walter not only keep his books straight, she also connects him with some finance people who help find the financing to buy some machines, hire more people, and move into a bigger facility.

He's then able to take on bigger projects, which brings him in front of bigger clients. One of those clients mentions to Walter that they need to shore up their disaster recovery plan, so Walter gives them your name, brags on the work you do, and they end up contacting you for your services.

And those people talk you up to their connections, and it keeps on going.

Basically, if you help enough people, you become the subject of conversations when you're not even in the room.

Erik has had this happen plenty of times, especially when he first started out in the social media world. In 2007, Erik had already been blogging for ten years and had cemented his reputation in Central Indiana as a blogging expert by publishing a daily humor article on his personal blog.[2]

He would regularly have coffee or lunch with other people and help them set up their own blogs. He would answer questions about blogging and social media. And he gave talks about blogging and social media to business groups and nonprofits.

In early 2009, he applied for a job at a content marketing agency, and the owner, Mike, refused to interview him.

"Just come work for me!" Mike said. "I know what you can do; *everyone* knows what you can do. Whenever I tell people what I do, your name always comes up. Just come work for me."

Erik became the owner of the agency six months later, but that's a story for another time. (And no, it did not involve a coup.)

It happened because Erik had made his reputation and established his value by helping people with a

---

[2] https://ErikDeckers.com, if you're curious

new method of communication and promotion. He was always happy to share his knowledge with other people and help them get started. As a result, it set his entire career on an unexpected path, which he's still following today.

It came in the form of a lot of people mentioning his name in the rooms where he was not. And because enough people did that, Mike heard about him over and over, and conducted the shortest interview in Erik's job history.

The idea that "Blessings/Karma/Cool points will always come back even if it's not from the person I helped" holds true for anyone who adopts the Givers Gain mindset.

In essence, giving freely without expecting anything in return creates a ripple effect. It fosters goodwill and makes you an indispensable part of other people's networks. And it spreads your brand and reputation so even more people believe this about you without you ever meeting those people.

It's why you're even reading this book.

Bringing Value is Based on Relationships

No matter how talented or skilled you are, if your relationships aren't built on trust and mutual respect, your value will be limited.

In other words, people won't trust you enough to offer you opportunities until you have earned the right to bring value into their lives.

Which means **you build your reputation as a value creator on the foundation of your relationships**.

Questions to Ask in Finding Your Own Value

One of the most effective ways to build relationships is by asking the right questions when you first meet someone.

As mentioned before, Robert often asks people, "Who's a good customer for you?" He has found this to be a great way to unlock potential connections and business deals. By taking the time to understand what someone needs, he can position himself as a resource. Not just for the product he's selling, but as a connector and advisor to the person he's talking to.

Be careful, though: This requires genuine curiosity and a willingness to listen.

You're not just asking questions to further your own agenda; you're doing it to gain the insight needed to truly help someone else.

Another effective question is to ask, "Who are you looking to meet?"

This not only shows your willingness to help, it gives you the chance to leverage your existing network to create more introductions. The people who become connectors — the ones who can introduce valuable contacts and resources — are the ones who stand out at networking events. They're the ones that others want to be around because they're consistently opening doors for the people they meet.

Why Do People Want You at a Networking Event?

Robert is a strong example of someone who has mastered the art of becoming a magnet at networking events. As he talks with people, his focus isn't on getting something from every interaction.

Instead, he asks questions, offers help, and works to become a reliable presence. He follows up, builds trust, and does what he can to add value to every relationship. This is why people want him at their events — because he brings more to the room than just a business card.

When you bring your value to a room like that, people will naturally gravitate toward you. Your network will begin to see you as someone they want to be around, not because of what you need, but because of what you give.

The value you bring becomes your personal brand.

What's Your Motivation? Do You Have an Agenda or Ulterior Motive?

Another critical component of finding your value is your motivation behind what you're doing.

If your purpose in connecting with someone is to further your own interests, it will show. People can tell when you have an ulterior motive, and it can erode trust before a relationship even begins, and they won't want to connect with you.

A quick aside: This is also true for your job search. If you're desperate — *truly* desperate — to find a job and you're hoping to walk away from that interview with an offer in your hand, that vibe comes through, and the interviewers will pick up on it. Rather than throw you a lifeline and save you, they'll be turned off by it. The answer will be no, and you'll still be out searching.

In that same way, the "I wonder what this person can do for me" vibe comes through when you meet people.

It comes through when you talk about yourself more than you ask about the other person. Or when you don't look the other person in the eyes because you're constantly looking over their shoulder to see who else is there. Or when the first thing you do is hand them a business card.

When either of us goes to a networking event, our motivation is clear: "I want to add value for you."

Being transparent about your value-first mindset not only puts the other person at ease, it sets you apart from the people who are purely self-serving. Your goal should be to offer help, make connections, or provide insights. When people realize your intent is genuine, they'll be more inclined to trust you.

Find Opportunities for the Customer You Want

As we've discussed already, one of the best ways to bring value is to find opportunities for the people you want to work with. The best way to get it is by giving them business.

If you have a sales prospect, do everything you can to bring them value, whether it's through their own sales referrals, introductions to prospects, or even a chance to promote themselves to your own audience.

Erik knows several podcasters who use their podcast as a sales tool. The podcasters usually work in a specific industry and are trying to make their name in the field. But the primary goal of the podcast isn't just to be a good podcaster; it's to make sales for their company.

So, they treat their podcast as a lead generation tool.

Rather than making phone calls to get an appointment with a prospect, they instead invite that person to come onto their podcast and talk about their own business. This is a chance for that customer to share their story and their company with the podcaster's network and reach a (hopefully) few thousand people.

Later, when the prospect actually needs the thing the podcaster sells, they'll remember their time on the show, or they'll be more interested in taking that podcaster's call.

Now, it's important that the podcaster's motivation is not self-serving. They shouldn't be doing the podcast *in order to* make sales. Otherwise, just like desperation shows up in a job interview, the podcaster's motivation will be obvious to their listeners and their prospects.

If people realize they're being used, they won't trust you and refuse any efforts to build a relationship. Then, when the podcaster realizes their efforts aren't successful, they'll quit doing it. But those people who are actually motivated to provide value are more likely to be successful.

So if you know someone who is looking for a specific kind of customer, and you have someone in your network who fits that profile — or has more of that kind of customer in their own network — make the introduction.

Set Yourself Apart Through Communication

Of course, the easiest way to communicate with people is electronically. But you can stand apart from most people just by communicating with them at all beyond a simple text or email asking for something.

For example, sending someone an article with a "this made me think of you" message makes you stand out from everyone else. You haven't asked for anything, you don't want anything. You're just sharing something to be helpful.

But there are two old-school ways to stand head and shoulders above the electronic communicators.

Robert loves sending handwritten cards to people he's meeting out in the field. He was once in his company's main office, and he asked his chief financial officer, "Where is our stationery? I want to write some handwritten cards to our customers I meet in the field."

The CFO took him to the supply closet and said, "I know you're old school and like to do these. I remember receiving two of them from you when you were interviewing for this position."

That's because Robert has made it a regular practice to send someone a handwritten card whenever he meets with someone. That helps him stand out because very few people mail handwritten cards anymore.

But Erik has found a way to help him stand head and shoulders above the handwritten card crowd: a manual typewriter. Two typewriters, in fact. One from 1953 and another from 1935. He also printed half-sheet letterhead with only his name, email, and phone number on it.

After an important meeting or great sales call, or even when he just wants to wow somebody, he will type out a short note on his letterhead and mail it to the other person.

On nearly every occasion, he has received a phone call or email back from the other person raving about the fact that someone sent them a *typed* message. (One person even put it on their refrigerator.) In most cases, the people he sends the typed messages to are old enough to have used a typewriter themselves, and the sense of nostalgia is powerful.

For others, it's a brand-new experience that they've never had before. (Another recipient thought it was a printer font and was flabbergasted to learn it had been done on a real typewriter.)

Ultimately, the most successful relationships are built on mutual value. When you make it your mission to help others achieve their goals, you not only bring value to them, you position yourself as someone they want to have in their network.

By focusing on relationships and understanding the needs of others, you bring value to other people, and your personal brand is built around that. It becomes sustainable and scalable because the more people you help, the more your own brand will spread to their own networks.

Chapter 4
The Importance
of Networking

In the last chapter, we talked a lot about how you bring value to people's lives and how that's especially going to happen during networking events. That could be your local chamber of commerce, an event for your particular job title or industry, a social club, a special interest group, or one of the many, many — *so* many — business networking groups that you can find on Meetup and other event-based websites.

Networking is the best and fastest way to build your brand in a way that provides value to others. Remember, it's not about what you can take, but what you can give. It's also a question of quality of contacts over quantity. But you can either try to meet people one at a time through random chance, or you can put yourself in situations where you meet several people at a time on a regular basis and speed up the meeting-people process.

When you approach networking with a philosophy of generosity and giving, people will notice that and learn to trust you. That starts with asking people what you can do for them, who you can introduce them to, and what kind of customers they would like to meet. It's *not* about trying to figure out what they can do for you.

We talked about this in chapter three, but we need to reiterate it because so many people get it wrong. Plus, you may have skipped that chapter and landed here first. We don't know you, and we wouldn't presume to tell you how to read a book.

Most people do networking all wrong. They think it's about collecting business cards, promoting their products, and pushing their own personal agenda. But the real power of networking comes from creating opportunities for others first.

Givers gain, people! Givers gain!

(OK, go back and read chapter three first, if you haven't already.)

Networking Tactics for You to Try

How you network is just as important as *whether* you network. If you had to choose between only doing one method or not doing it at all, the one method is going to bring you much more success than waiting for opportunities to fall into your lap.

But you can increase your chances of success and make things more efficient if you try more than one tactic. They don't all take the same amount of time, and some of them only need to be done once every few weeks. But if you do these things, you can stand out among your new contacts, and they'll remember you more because you're consistent, persistent, and even a little bold.

Face-to-Face Networking Over Social Media

When email became popular, the use of regular snail mail and faxing plummeted. Similarly, face-to-face meetings dropped when social media and Zoom calls became popular. (Of course, we also blame Covid for that.)

It might seem like face-to-face networking isn't as important as it used to be or that attending in-person events is less important. But meeting people in person can elevate your brand in ways that online connections never will. While everyone else may be satisfied with virtual and social connections, you can stand out by sticking with the face-to-face, eye-to-eye meetings where you shake hands and share space.

Robert's daughter is an Instagram influencer with (as of this writing 1 million followers. But even with a massive online audience, she still networks in person. She doesn't only work on her phone, she makes sure to meet people in real life. Attending events gives her new opportunities to grow her audience, connect with brands, and collaborate with other influencers.

By showing up, meeting people, and getting real-world photos for her social media work, her face-to-face networking directly strengthens her online presence.

In a lot of ways, this is how entrepreneurship works. Part of the time, you're doing the work that you get paid for, and then in the other part, you're building your business through sales, marketing, and networking.

For Erik, face-to-face networking transformed his career early on. In 2007, when he lived in Indianapolis, he started attending multiple networking events every week, sometimes two or three in one day. A morning event, a networking lunch, and a business after-hours event at one of the local chambers of commerce.

This helped him build trust in the local Indiana marketing community as he was seen everywhere and was meeting a lot of people. He also joined a startup social network called Smaller Indiana (now defunct) and participated regularly.

As a result, he not only became a familiar face, he became one of the leading authorities of digital marketing and personal branding in the Midwest. It ultimately gave him the cachet and reputation to be asked to ghostwrite a Twitter marketing book, and then follow that up with two more books on social media marketing and personal branding.

These events gave him opportunities to meet decision-makers, connect with other professionals, and establish himself as a reliable resource. People remembered him not only because of what he did or how he made them feel, they remembered him because he showed up regularly.

People do business with people they know and trust. Face-to-face interactions allow you to show up as your authentic self. You can listen, engage, and create genuine connections that go far beyond a LinkedIn request or an email introduction.

Social networking over face-to-face networking

We know social media is critical. We're not going to tell you that face-to-face networking is better than social media. (Or vice versa.)

Erik built his own career writing about using social media to build your personal brand. And while he laments what it has become — and sometimes feels embarrassed for being one of the people who contributed to that — he still believes in the power of social media because it can do so many things that face-to-face networking just can't.

- **It's scalable.** How many people can you truly meet and have meaningful conversations with at a networking event? About four, tops. Otherwise, you're just racing around and shaking hands, but not having real conversations. On a social network, you can speak to hundreds and thousands of people. Maybe not as meaningfully as in-person, but you're making lots of small contacts over a long period, not one long one. Those add up.

- **It's international.** You may find people to collaborate and connect with halfway around the world. You're not limited to only the people who are in that room at that moment. Erik's younger daughter belongs to an artist's Discord channel with participants from the Netherlands, France, and Australia.

- **It's asynchronous.** Synchronous communication is when both parties are involved in the conversation at the same time, like a phone call. Asynchronous means "not in sync.' You can communicate and answer at different times, like email. On social media, you can respond and chat at any time, even a couple days later.

- **It lets you target only the people you want to connect with.** It's so easy to find people who share your interests, work in your field, or have the same job as you. Maybe you want to meet people who like to cosplay anime characters, or you want to meet other writers or other salespeople. Maybe you want only those who work in alternative energy finance. With social media, you can find exactly who you want and connect with them, no matter where they live.

- **It's measurable.** Thirty years ago, when you did marketing and advertising, the best you could say about the results was that they were a complete guess. Sure, you could count things like the number of people who redeemed a paper coupon, but how many people actually read your postcard or watched your TV commercial? You could never find out. Social media is completely measurable, and you can tell if you're getting the traction and attention you need on a particular platform.

Even if you consider yourself a people person who favors meeting someone face-to-face, looking them in the eye, and shaking their hand, social media lets you deepen relationships with fast interactions that take seconds instead of longer meetings over lunch over coffee.

You can sometimes learn more things about a person through social media interactions than you can by talking in person.

Introduce people
As we said in the previous chapter, the most successful networkers focus on helping each

other. When Robert and Erik go to networking events, their goal is not to talk about their respective businesses; it's to find ways to connect people.

(Would you believe we've only ever been to four networking meetings together? The first one was where we met each other, which led to this book. The next three came after we realized that and decided to remedy that situation.)

Here's how you make introductions at a networking event:

You go to a networking event, start chatting with someone, and ask the obligatory questions: What's your name? What do you do? How long have you been doing that? Who are you looking to meet?

Then, you'll separate and go on to meet new people, asking the same questions. And invariably, someone will say they work in the same field as the first person you met. Or they want to meet someone like them. Or they want to meet the same kinds of customers.

Drag this person (metaphorically, not literally) to find the previous person you were talking to. Introduce them and explain to each of them what the other person does. You can even explain why you want them to meet.

This has the added bonus of showing both of them that you were listening to them during your brief chat, and have already been thinking of ways you can help them.

Then, step away and let them talk, heading off in search of the next introduction you can make.

If you really want to get a lot out of an in-person networking event, make it your goal to introduce as many people as you can at the event. Find the people who are looking for a particular kind of person and then find their match. Act like a business matchmaking service and make that your mission. As you do it, people will notice and start doing the same, creating their own habits of making introductions.

Make email introductions

The only thing easier than personal introductions is email introductions. They take just a few minutes, and the need to do them will only come up once in a while, although you're encouraged to do as many as you can.

Let's say you're meeting with someone, and you realize you need to connect them with someone else you know. They could both be local to you, or they could live several hours away from each other. The only way you're going to connect them is through email.

Email introductions are going to be one of the most powerful tools you have in your personal branding arsenal. The best way to do it is to write an email to both people at the same time, introduce them to each other, and explain why they should connect.

A basic email introduction goes like this:

> *Dena, meet Rajit. He owns a cybersecurity firm specializing in healthcare practices, including dentists, chiropractors, and optometrists. I met Rajit several years ago when he set up my company's cybersecurity system.*
>
> *Rajit, meet Dena. She is the office manager for a medical practice in Savannah, Georgia. I met her while I was on vacation last week.*
>
> *Dena was telling me during our conversation that her practice narrowly foiled a hacking attempt, thanks in part to their Internet Service Provider. They set her up with some increased security practices, but recommended that she find a better permanent fix.*
>
> *While Dena was telling me about this, I thought of Rajit and promised to connect you both when I got home. I'll leave it to you to find time to talk and see if there's*

> *a way you can help each other. Good luck!*

In just 141 words, Dena and Rajit know who each other are, they know the reason for the introduction, and how/why we made it. And by doing it through email, we've made sure to give each other their contact information, and explain how we want them to help each other. We didn't ask for anything in return, we didn't make them promise to owe us a favor, and we even stepped out of the way to let them continue the conversation.

More importantly, we didn't tell Dena to just email Rajit, or to tell Rajit to just call Dena. While Rajit, the business owner, might not mind a random potential customer emailing them, Dena might not want some random salesperson calling her. But by making the mutual introduction this way, we have, in essence, vouched for both of them. They both carry our little stamp of approval: We have said, "I know this person, and I can vouch for them. I believe in them enough to recommend them to you."

That makes them more likely to trust each other and more likely to work together.

Nothing may come of it, but at the same time, this could be a big deal and a major career moment for both of them. Dena could solve a major headache for her employer, which could boost her reputation as a problem-solver, and Dena's employer could turn out to be a large medical practice, making this a big sale for Rajit.

But remember, they don't owe us anything for the introduction. We just introduced them because we're connectors. We didn't ask for a returned favor, we didn't ask to be kept in the loop. In fact, we stepped out of the way and let them work it out for themselves.

Although we wouldn't say no to some cookies.

Host luncheons or mastermind groups

We're stealing this idea from Keith Ferrazzi, author of *Never Eat Alone* and *Who's Got Your Back?*.

A great way to build an interconnected network is to bring several of your friends/contacts/associates together at once and introduce them to each other. You can do this over lunch or even in a regular mastermind group.

With a special luncheon (Ferrazzi recommends a dinner), you would bring together seven other people who you think would have interesting conversations and come up with amazing ideas. Ferrazzi recommends getting people from completely different jobs and industries, like having a musician, a teacher, an engineer, and an architect at the same event.

Then, you throw out a couple topics of discussion, like asking, "How did you choose to go into your field?" or "How did your education prepare you for the work you do?" Each person will have their own stories, of course, but you'll be surprised to see how many parallels and coincidences come out because of this discussion.

People went to the same schools, or they were in the same major, or they know some of the same people. These connections will help them deepen those connections, and you may end up kicking off several friendships or collaborations that continue on long past your dinner.

When Erik lived in Indianapolis, he belonged to a mastermind group of marketing professionals who were competitors on paper. But, as part of the group, they all agreed to a few rules, including never stealing a client and each focusing on a particular niche to avoid overlap and competition. (This way, the competitors actually became good referral partners for one another.)

This practice also helped people form relationships and collaborations, and it gave everyone an insight into who they should call when they needed help with a client, such as a web developer who needed someone to write copy for a new website, or a direct mail marketer who needed a graphic designer.

Make referrals

Referrals are the lifeblood of networking — they're the whole reason you should be networking in the first place. Basically, you want people to think of you when someone asks them, "Do you know anyone who can help me with _____?"

A good referral is worth more than a dozen cold calls or pitches. That email introduction we wrote above? That's basically a referral, and it will probably work because it comes with built-in trust. When someone refers you to a potential client, they're putting their own reputation on the line.

That's why it's so important to deliver five-star work when someone refers you: You're not only protecting your own reputation, you're protecting the reputation of your friend who made the referral. Failing to deliver not only hurts your reputation, it hurts the trust others have in the person who referred you. That's why we're both careful about who we refer people to.

Don't forget to ask for referrals and recommendations, either. Tools like LinkedIn and Alignable allow people to provide public recommendations, which are powerful for building your credibility. Just remember to provide exceptional value and build strong relationships before you ask for them. You can't just demand them, you have to earn them. That's what makes them so valuable.

Ask smart questions

Effective networking isn't about talking, it's about listening. You need to make sure you're practicing active listening when you're talking to someone, but we'll leave that for another book.

Instead, we'll tell you to ask intentional questions that help you understand the other person's goals. Once you get to know what they do, ask them deeper questions like:

- Can you walk me through your process?
- What challenges are you facing right now?
- Who do you need to meet to grow your business?
- What made you get into this line of work?
- Who was a mentor when you were coming up in the industry?
- Do you listen to any podcasts about your industry?

Questions like these show that you're interested in helping them, not selling to them.

Focus on asking them questions and listening, rather than falling for the trap of talking too much about yourself. As we keep saying, you're not there to sell your own product or share your own achievements. If you want to stand out at a networking event, focus on asking good questions and listening, and people will remember you as someone who made them feel heard and valued.

Build Relational Equity

Remember, networking isn't a short-term game, it's about building relational equity. But here's the key: You have to make a lot of deposits before you can ever make a withdrawal.

You do that by showing up consistently. Attend events, connect people to each other, and offer value without expecting anything in return. Ask them smart questions and listen to the answers.

Follow up with the people you meet, especially with hand-written or typed notes to say thank you or to share a resource you promised.

Networking is one of the most powerful tools for building your personal brand. It's the way you create relationships based on trust, value, and integrity.

When you do networking with the right mindset, it becomes more than just a business tool. It's possibly *the* most effective way to elevate your personal brand.

Chapter 5
Giving to Gain

One of the best ways to grow your personal brand is just by helping others without expecting anything in return.

This is more than Givers Gain, though. You're not just making a referral on someone's behalf or introducing them to a potential customer. It's about giving your time, skills, and knowledge freely, and maybe for a longer term than just that single introduction.

Your plan is not just to help them by being generous, you're investing in a long-term relationship that could lead to opportunities that you never expected.

Back in the early 1990s, when Erik was first starting out in marketing in a small business (a poultry equipment exporting company), he developed a print brochure — his first ever! — for a new product the company was getting ready to sell. He took a draft print to the print shop they were going to use, someone he had never met, let alone worked with.

To say this brochure was not very good is an understatement; it was terrible. But the print shop owner, Mike, was kind, and he took. . . let's call it pity on Erik. He showed him how to design a better, more eye-catching brochure. He explained some design basics and his print capabilities to help him better understand what the brochure should actually look like.

Needless to say, Erik's next effort was much better, and they ended up printing several thousand copies of the brochure. Not only that, but Erik and Mike became friends. They sent a lot more print business Mike's way and even referred other prospects to him. Mike even joined Erik on his annual fishing trip to Canada one year.

The point of the story is that Mike invested a lot of time into Erik at the beginning of their relationship, and it turned into a long-lasting business relationship as well as a friendship. Mike said later that he could have just printed what Erik wanted and not spent several hours teaching him about print and graphic design. But he knew that if he invested the time, it would have reaped greater rewards later on, which it did.

This idea of "giving to gain" is still based on providing value to others before asking for anything for yourself. (Maybe even never ask for anything for yourself — just trust that it will come.) But it's about making a bigger investment into that relationship.

It's a mentoring relationship or a coaching relationship. Or you're helping out a growing company by serving as an advisor.

This isn't a transactional relationship, it's about creating trust and building a reputation as someone who adds long-term value to the people and organizations they work with. And the rewards that you reap will be emotionally, professionally, personally, and possibly financially fulfilling.

You may even get to go fishing.

Be a Servant First

Giving to gain (and Givers Gain, for that matter) means helping people get what they want. In the regular Givers Gain philosophy, it's a matter of doing things that people need to help them succeed, but what we're talking about now is going a step beyond that.

Whatever you call it — Servant Leadership, volunteering, Super Givers Gain — means going above and beyond what we've discussed in previous chapters. You're going to get more involved in people's lives and become an important part of what they do.

This is a sowing and reaping philosophy that, if you plant enough seeds deeply enough, you will reap untold rewards.

Robert lives by this principle by mentoring startups and young entrepreneurs for free, even when his schedule is packed. Why? Because he knows that investing a few hours in someone else's success can pay off in surprising ways.

For example, mentoring startups might lead to one becoming a client, or one of them might offer him equity in their business. Or maybe a founder of one that didn't succeed will find themselves in need of Robert's services a few years later when they're in a different role.

He doesn't know which of those seeds will grow into opportunities, but he trusts that his efforts will pay off. And if they don't, he's also added to his personal brand with other people. That is, if *they* see him helping the original groups, they may consider asking him to help with their own work.

It doesn't even have to be on the business side of things when it comes to helping others get what they want. Volunteering for a nonprofit or serving on a board will also help you achieve this. We'll talk about that further in this chapter.

Ultimately, the goal is to create long-term value for everyone involved.

Think Long-Term, Not Transactional

Giving isn't about instant gratification; it's about strategic long-term payoffs. Helping someone today won't result in an immediate return, but it sets the stage for bigger and better opportunities later on.

One of Erik's community involvements is with the Kerouac Project of Orlando, a writing residency and the home where Jack Kerouac (author of *On The Road*) lived in 1957 and 1958 when he wrote *The Dharma Bums*. Erik is the president of the board of directors, and he was also the Spring 2016 writer-in-residence. As president, he's invested countless hours into the nonprofit, helping to preserve a historic home and providing a space for writers to work on their craft.

This might seem like plain old volunteerism, but the reality is that Erik's connection to one of the world's most famous writing residencies has elevated his personal brand and given him cachet in certain circles — Orlando's literary scene and the local nonprofit community as well.

Being associated with an important cultural institution has opened doors for speaking gigs, new contacts, and media invitations, as well as cemented his reputation as a writer of note.

This wasn't his purpose in joining the board back in late 2016 or stepping into the president's role in 2022. They have been the serendipitous byproducts of the work he has done. Instead, by focusing on helping others achieve their goals, he has naturally aligned yourself with people and opportunities that can elevate his own brand and improve his reputation. The key is to focus on the long game — doing the things that you're good at and make you happy — not getting the short-term rewards.

Giving to Get Access

There's one key place where this strategy can really pay off, and that's when you want to meet someone who can offer bigger opportunities or rewards.

We call this the Person Zero Strategy: look for the key person in an organization or someone who is already successful and then offer them something of value: helping them organize a conference, volunteering for their nonprofit, or just arranging introductions and connections for them.

Back when Erik worked for the same poultry equipment company we mentioned earlier, they attended the International Poultry Expo in Atlanta every year, the most important poultry show in the world. In their first year in the show, they managed to get a booth on the main floor through sheer luck. Erik was the marketing director, which meant he was in charge of all trade shows.

Seeing that they had been given a huge gift, Erik made it a point to get to know the show organizer, Ed, during the show, walking the floor with him during his downtime, and even getting lunch one day. A few months later, when it was time to start thinking about their booth for the next year, Erik called Ed with a proposition: "If you can get us a larger peninsula booth, I'll fill it with four other exhibitors, and I'll manage all of their paperwork so you only have to deal with one of us."

Ed set them up in a prime spot in the front of the main hall, and Erik managed the displays for all five exhibitors. They had this arrangement for several years, until Erik's employer closed down. Erik was even invited to serve on the expo's advisory committee for a few years, flying down to Atlanta a couple of times to advise on future shows.

This same principle applies to speaking opportunities, for example. If you want to speak at a conference, start by helping the organizers and volunteering for the conference itself. Offer to write promotional materials, assist with logistics, help secure sponsors, and so on. Once you have proven your value, it's much easier to ask for a speaking slot. People are far more likely to say yes to someone who has already shown they're a team player.

This isn't limited to conferences, though. If you want to join a board, volunteer for their events. If you want to connect with a high-roller or high-net-worth individual, volunteer for the nonprofit they're on the board of. If you want to work for a particular company, connect with your potential boss and support the company publicly, whether it's through social media, referrals, or other means.

Just by showing up and offering value, you'll often gain access to the opportunities you're looking for and then some.

Share Networking Opportunities With Connections

We've already talked about how to find networking opportunities — Eventbrite, Meetup, LinkedIn, and your local chamber of commerce, just to name a few. Check for local events regularly, bookmark the most promising ones, and then attend the ones you can. Be sure to put them on your calendar right away.

(One tip is to save all the event page URLs of your area chambers and networking groups into a single folder on your browser. Then, save the folder in your bookmark bar, click the folder, and all the pages will open at once.)

After you attend a few events, you'll start receiving regular updates from the different groups you're a part of. That makes it easier to stay in the loop. And the more you show up, the more people you'll meet, and the more opportunities will come your way.

Build a networking posse

But it doesn't stop there: One unique strategy Robert has been developing is to create a "networking posse."

This is a small group of people who share information about events and opportunities with each other. Robert sends individual texts to people in his network, as well as posts to his LinkedIn page, about the events he's attending. He'll also ask where they'll be and if they're going to attend the events themselves.

This approach has helped him stay connected and meet new people without relying on impersonal group texts. The idea is that when he shares what he knows, others will do the same. For example, if Robert finds out about an exclusive event, he'll text a few trusted contacts to let them know. In turn, they'll share opportunities with them. This creates a constant flow of information that benefits everyone involved.

The beauty of this approach is its flexibility. You don't need a formal system or a large group. Even just a handful of trusted connections can make a big difference. The important thing is to be proactive and intentional about sharing opportunities.

The Power of Mentorship

Mentorship is a natural extension of giving, so it's important to discuss it here.

(That, and we didn't know where else to put it.)

When you mentor someone, you're investing in their growth and success. Whether you mentor a company, an entrepreneur, or a young person who's still learning the ropes. It's one of the most rewarding ways to give back, and it often leads to unexpected opportunities.

Both Robert and Erik mentor young executives and entrepreneurs regularly. We listen to their challenges, offer advice, and connect them with people who can help.

For example, Rob has mentored one young executive, Caleb, who created a personal board of directors, including Robert, to guide him through his business decisions. By giving his time and expertise, and most importantly, making himself available whenever Caleb needs it, he's able to help Caleb stretch himself and achieve greater goals than what he originally intended.

Erik has mentored a young entrepreneur, Sean, for more than 13 years, starting when Sean was just finishing college. He's helped him find jobs, learn to network and connect with others, and grow professionally and personally. Along the way, Sean has also been able to help Erik with different parts of his own professional life, including hiring Erik for writing work.

We both have enjoyed mentoring our young friends — dozens of them over the years — and we have developed deep friendships with the people we've worked with. It has been immensely rewarding and something we certainly recommend to anyone of any age.

In fact, mentorship is not just for older professionals mentoring younger ones. There is no reason that an older professional shouldn't have younger people mentoring them on things like social media, technology, or emerging trends.

Mentors of any age should have mentors of any age, especially when you reach the advanced years that we have, and your normal older mentors have retired or passed on. You don't reach the age and stage where you know everything and have nothing left to learn.

So if you're a younger professional, this can be your way to connect with Person Zero to get important access to them: ask them if there's something they would like to learn or that you could teach them. Even if it's just helping them figure something out on their phone, a small favor can lead to a big opportunity.

Everyone has something to teach, regardless of age or professional achievements. By being open to learning from younger generations, older professionals can stay relevant and adapt to a rapidly changing world.

The Law of Sowing and Reaping

At its core, this whole chapter is about sowing and reaping.

When you give freely, you're planting seeds that will grow into opportunities. If you only plant one, you may not get anything. But the more seeds you plant, the more that will grow into opportunities.

Sometimes the rewards come directly from the person you helped; other times, they come from unexpected places. But they do come.

Just remember that you don't have to plant hundreds of seeds over and over by making email introductions and referrals. Sometimes, you need to "Super Give" in order to gain deeper results. Join boards, volunteer, get involved, and mentor others. Associate yourself with doing good in your community and build your brand and reputation by helping others. It's a great way to learn, connect, and show what you know.

Chapter 6
Integrity is the Core of Your Brand

Every relationship we have, whether it's with our parents, romantic partner, business associates, or even our favorite grocery store or coffee shop, is built on trust. We trust our parents to care for us, our partners to love us, our business associates to tell the truth, our grocery store to charge fair prices, and our coffee shop to not serve us decaf in the mornings.

Without trust, there is no foundation for a meaningful connection, whether it's in your personal or your business life.

When we talk about personal branding, we're talking about your reputation. Remember the "oh, good" or "oh, s#!t!" response? People say "oh, good" if they can trust you and know they can count on you.

Your reputation is built on integrity — saying what you do and doing what you say, staying true to your values, and keeping your word. Integrity leads to trust, and that's what builds lasting relationships.

Without integrity, you're always searching for the next sucker, constantly replacing people who see through you.

That's not only an unsustainable way to build a career, it's a terrible way to go through life.

Years ago, when Erik worked for his father-in-law's poultry equipment company (see Chapter 5), they had a dealer — let's call him Bill — in Georgia who stuck them with unpaid invoices totaling more than $25,000 ($50,000 in 2025 dollars). The company filed a lawsuit against Bill and had a summons served by the sheriff's deputy for the total amount.

Bill declared bankruptcy for his company, avoided paying what he owed the company, and started a new company under a different name. It turns out, this was Bill's regular habit: he would keep everything from the sales he brokered, rack up tens of thousands of dollars of debt, declare bankruptcy, and start a new company. It was totally legal, but it was the company that went bankrupt and out of business, not the owner.

So Erik's company did what any company that had been ripped off would do: They warned anyone they saw having a conversation with Bill about what he had done, and they were able to save a few other small companies from getting stuck with unpaid invoices. Bill ultimately left the industry because so many people learned about his dishonesty and complete lack of integrity that he was never able to work in that field again.

The Power of Integrity

It's not only important that you yourself have integrity; it's important that your company has it as well. If your company shows that it hires and works with people of integrity, and you show your integrity when you don't have to or when you're in a crisis, people are more likely to trust you and stay loyal to you when you need it most.

Once, when Robert had joined a company as a and EVP, a sales rep had discovered they had not received commissions on a large account worth $130,000 in sales. This situation existed before Robert joined the company, but as a leader, he had a choice.

He could either ignore the problem and protect the company's finances, or he could honor the agreement they had with the sales rep and make things right.

Robert chose to honor the company's commitment despite resistance from leadership. They wanted to protect their finances, but Robert stood by the written agreement because he knew that trust and integrity are priceless. He also knew that you can't put a price on your brand, although a plaintiff's attorney is certainly willing to try.

More importantly, he realized that if a brand is built on integrity, you have to do what's right, even when it might hurt in the short term. The benefits in the long term will more than outweigh the damage.

Your personal brand isn't just what you do for a living — it's the kind of person you are and the way you behave, especially when you think no one is paying attention. Or, more importantly, when the person you made a commitment to doesn't have any power to hurt you.

Because people notice when you're someone they can trust. Because that trust opens doors that your skills and connections cannot.

And because if enough people hear about you hurting or taking advantage of someone for a small thing, they'll never trust you with the big things.

The Role of Trust in Branding

Trust is at the heart of every corporate brand, as we mentioned. People gravitate toward the companies they believe in and the ones that have done right by them.

Consider the outdoor clothing and equipment company, Patagonia, which built trust in its products by focusing on sustainability from it. Sustainability has been Yvon Chouinard's watchword since 1957, when he learned how to make his own rock climbing pitons. He built better pitons than his European counterparts, so his pitons became wildly successful and became 70% of his fledgling company, Chouinard Equipment.

But he realized that those same pitons were damaging rock faces by the climbers who used them, something he saw for himself. Rather than shrugging his shoulders, he quit making the pitons altogether and began making a replacement called chocks.

To build trust in those among his climbing compatriots, he used them to ascend the north face of El Capitan, the vertical rock formation in Yosemite National Park. Within a few years, the chocks had replaced the pitons, and he had redefined the entire sport of rock climbing.

Chouinard and Patagonia (which he formed in 1973) have made several painful decisions that made it more difficult and expensive to produce their clothing, such as switching all of their clothing line (166 products) to organic cotton in

1994.[3] It was painful, it cost a lot of money, and cut deeply into their profits, but they knew they had to honor their commitment to saving the planet.

The same principle applies to personal branding. If you consistently provide value, keep your word, and show that you're reliable, people will trust you. This trust will lead to stronger relationships, more opportunities, and a better reputation. But if you are inconsistent or self-serving, people will pay attention, trust will erode, and your opportunities will plummet.

This is something Erik learned from his father-in-law, Carmon, who was his business mentor for many years. Carmon used to say that he was friends with his equipment dealers around the world, and they all knew he would rather lose a deal than lose a friend.

Carmon always did what he could to protect his dealers, especially when there was a factory or shipping error. He always took care of the dealers and made sure they didn't lose money on a supplier's or shipper's mistake, even when the supplier/shipper did everything they could to avoid taking the blame and losing money themselves.

---

[3] Read Patagonia's story at https://www.patagonia.com/stories/how-we-got-here-organic-cotton/story-97024.html.

This accomplished two things:

1) It ensured that neither Carmon nor the dealer would ever use that supplier or shipper again. After all, they showed who they were and how trustworthy they were, so why would anyone want to risk getting taken advantage of again?

2) It showed the dealer that Carmon would protect them, even when it hurt his own profits. In return, they would either offer to share the burden and split the costs, or they would make it up with a bigger order the next time. Either way, Carmon ended up making more money as a "thank you" than he would have if he had tried to grab everything for himself one time.

As a result, everyone in the industry knew they could trust Carmon and that he would honor his commitments to the people he did business with. Even his competitors respected him and would sometimes offer a hand in a pinch.

Once, when Erik and Carmon were at a conference in the Netherlands, Carmon had forgotten his wallet. One of Carmon's long-time rivals and toughest competitors saw that they were in distress and offered to cover the bill because he knew Carmon would pay him back the next morning. Luckily, Erik remembered his, and everything was fine. But it showed that even

Carmon's bitterest rivals trusted and respected him.

Building trust takes time, honesty, transparency, and consistency. If you make a mistake, own it, apologize, and fix it or make up for it. If you commit to something, follow through with it. If you openly share your thought processes and reasons about things like price increases, customers will be more likely to accept them. (But don't blame inflation and then give your executives million-dollar bonuses.)

Over time, your actions will define who you are and make you someone people will trust and recommend. As you continue to do this over the years, you will have a well-earned and widespread reputation as someone that people can turn to when they need help.

Having Integrity on Social Media

Your social media presence has an impact on your integrity as well. Not only does it offer opportunities to showcase your expertise, but you can share your values as well. However, this is also where you can damage your brand if you don't use it carefully.

You can show which side you fall on in certain important issues — Crunchy or smooth peanut butter? Should mayonnaise go on a hamburger? Is a hot dog a sandwich? — and show support for the causes you believe in.

(Crunchy. Yes. Yes. We will brook no arguments.)

But if you're inconsistent, unprofessional, or negative online, that can undermine the trust you've built elsewhere. If you're an argumentative jerk who feels they have to "well, actually" someone else's social media posts, that's who people are going to see you as. It doesn't matter how you behave in person or how you treat people in the real world. If your only interaction with people is on social media, this is going to be the version of you they understand.

That means you need to leave politics out of your social media life. It doesn't matter how strongly you feel about your side or your favorite politician; just know that roughly half of your potential audience does not agree with you. And a large number of people will refuse to do business with you if they think you support The Other Side.

That doesn't mean you shouldn't share your ideas or things you support, but avoid denigrating the things that other people like. If you like Taylor Swift, don't bash the people who don't. And if you don't like Taylor Swift, don't share social media posts about how much you hate her. Because that hiring manager or buyer may be a huge Swiftie, and your negative post could ruin your chances of working with that person.

Does it seem petty to make a decision over a personal preference? Absolutely! There's no question. Does that render that person's decision invalid? Not at all. They're free to make any decision they want and then say it was because of something else.

Does that mean you have to be fake and put up a false front?

Absolutely not. Remember, social media is about adding value through insightful posts, helpful advice, relatable stories, and asking questions and providing answers. You can do all of that without denigrating a political candidate or beloved entertainer.

You can post about the things you do like without smacking down the things you don't like.

Treat your online identity as an extension of your professional identity. Share content that aligns with your values and expertise. Avoid controversy unless it directly relates to your brand.

For example, Erik is not only a professional writer and a college professor, he's also a newspaper humor columnist. A lot of the things he writes are funny[4], not just the weekly columns. So, being funny even while he's being educational and informative is part of his brand. That means he'll post something humorous and smart-alecky on social media without being crude or offensive.

That's just his brand, and people know that if they work with him, he'll be as humorous when they work with him. He's living his brand by posting humorous things as well as serious things.

Robert is a consummate networker and connector. So, the things he posts on social media all have to do with the networking events he's attending or network advice he wants to share. This isn't a front he puts on to make people think he's well-connected; he actually *is* that well-connected. He doesn't just want people to think he reads a lot of information on networking; he actually *does* read that much, and he's eager to share what he's learned with his online network.

Your digital messages reflect on you, so use social media as a tool to amplify the trust and integrity you want associated with your name.

The Power of the Handshake

One thing both Erik and Robert take very seriously is the handshake.

---

[4] He hopes.

It has been used since prehistory to demonstrate peaceful intent because it shows that the right hand holds no weapon. It's saying, "I mean you no harm. I will not fight you."

In fact, one of the earliest depictions of a handshake is from the 9th century BC. It's an Assyrian relief that shows the Assyrian king Shalmaneser III shaking the hand of the Babylonian king Marduk-zakir-shumi to seal an alliance. And we all know how that turned out.

Then, in the 18th and 19th centuries in Britain and other parts of Europe, handshaking gained in popularity among two groups: 1) The merchant community who used handshakes to confirm deals that crossed cultural and ethnic divides; and, 2) The Quakers who embraced handshaking as part of their belief in human equality.

These days, in addition to being a greeting that hearkens back to that "I'm unarmed" message, a handshake also symbolizes mutual agreement to a promise or commitment. You may have heard people say, "Let's shake on it," or seen them seal a deal with a verbal promise and handshake. This shows that they will honor their promises to one another.

In a sense, they will do no harm to their promise.

We shake hands when we meet someone for the first time, greet a long-time associate or friend, part ways, offer congratulations, or say thank you. Among athletes, it's a sign of good sportsmanship, offering congratulations or commiserations, and a way of offering respect to the person you just did battle with, parting as friends.

Ultimately, the handshake conveys trust and respect. In a way, it goes back to that promise of "I will not harm you." And for many people you interact with, this is the first step in how they get to know you in the first place.

A Note on Standing for Handshakes

While we're on the subject, one thing you should always do when you meet or greet someone is to stand up and shake their hand.

It's a sign of respect.

While it's not the social requirement it once was, and it's a little old school, it's still a notable practice. People will remember you because you stood up to meet them, especially if you always do this. Just like we recommended sending hand-written or hand-typed notes in previous chapters, people will remember this old-fashioned display of manners.

In the end, trust is still about reliability and integrity, although the methods we establish it have evolved. It's important that you're consistent both online and offline as a way to maintain a strong personal brand.

Chapter 7 Launch Your Personal Brand in the Corporate World

Building your personal brand while working a corporate job means walking a tightrope between establishing your industry expertise *outside* the company versus doing your actual job and keeping your boss happy.

It may seem like the two are in conflict — your boss may certainly see it that way — or you may believe that you're "not allowed" to do the one while you do the other, but think of it this way:

There are plenty of artists, musicians, writers, and hobbyists who work a day job. They work on the things they love in the evenings and on the weekends. It may be for enjoyment, or maybe that's how they made a second income. So why can't you do that with your own personal branding efforts? Why can't your side hustle be a hobby?*

(* *We recognize that a side hustle is not a "hobby" or anything as trivial.* It's eventually going to be your main source of income and the thing that takes you to the next level, professionally speaking.*)

(* *Of course, this is not to imply that hobbies are trivial or not worthy of respect. It's not like you're just sitting and watching TV or playing video games.**)

(* *And we're not saying watching TV and playing video games aren't—you know what? We're not going to keep doing this! Get back to reading!*)

But here's the important part: Your job is temporary, your personal brand is permanent. If you build it wisely, it will follow you long after you leave your current role. It may be the reputation that you earned in your company and in your industry, which enables you to find new opportunities at new companies within your industry. It may be the reputation you build in your "side hustle business," even while you're working for a company or in an industry you're not really a fan of.

Unless you're trying to build a reputation within your career industry, the real trick is to create a personal brand that exists independently of your employer while still making yourself more valuable within the company. Even if you *are* trying to build a reputation within your career industry, you still want your brand to exist outside of your company. The halo effect should come from you, not your employer.

If you do it right, your efforts won't just help your future career and your reputation; they will make you indispensable to your current company. But if things go south or if you decide you want something bigger, you can easily find new opportunities just by trading on the brand you have built.

Your Brand Follows You Everywhere

Remember, your personal brand isn't just about social media posts and networking events; it's every interaction you have, every project you finish, and every impression you make on other people. Each one builds on the next. If people associate you with reliability, expertise, and innovation, you have a strong, positive brand.

But if you're known for missing deadlines, cutting corners, and being difficult to work with, no amount of networking and social media will ever fix that.

Here are three ways you can strengthen your reputation at work.

Be reliable. If you consistently meet your deadlines, exceed your expectations, and deliver high-quality work, people will trust you.

Reliability is one of the strongest foundations for your personal brand. It means that when you speak, people will know you back up your words with actions. And if your boss or colleagues can count on you, they're more likely to support your branding efforts instead of questioning them.

Share knowledge. One of the fastest ways to establish yourself as a thought leader is to share what you know. Give away the good stuff! This doesn't mean acting like the smartest person in the room, it means being generous with your expertise.

Mentor junior employees, write training materials, provide training sessions, and give presentations at company meetings. When you help others grow, you're seen as a leader, and that's an important part of building a strong personal brand.

You don't have to be in a leadership position to do these things. You don't need the title of manager or director to start teaching others or sharing materials. Doing this of your own volition will help you look like a leader in other people's eyes.

Ask your department manager if you can train new employees or deliver a presentation on a new piece of software or process. Deliver a lunch-and-learn on a personal topic. Organize after-work events like volunteer opportunities or a company softball team.

Maintain integrity. Building a personal brand on deception, playing office politics, or taking credit for others' work will only cause you to crash and burn. You'll be known as *that* kind of person, and you'll never shake that off. That reputation will follow you around, especially as your colleagues' own professional networks grow. They'll meet someone who knows you or is considering hiring you, and they'll ask about your reputation and work style; your colleagues will be more than happy to share what you have done in the past.

Sometimes, it will be a spill-the-gory-details story that goes on for hours. Other times, it may just be a narrowing of the eyes and a slight head shake to subtly warn the other person. But the Internet and social media are filled with story after story of someone who was able to torpedo the job prospects of an old manager or colleague who had tried to hurt them professionally.

While it's never a good idea to gossip or talk about someone behind their back — that's not a sign of integrity either — it's also never a good idea to fail to warn a friend from entering into a bad relationship when you know you could save them.

Always be honest, transparent, and ethical in your relationships, both personal and professional. If you're known for being fair, trustworthy, and the kind of person who builds people up, your brand will have long-term staying power. People remember those who have operated with integrity, and they'll be more likely to help you transition to higher roles and new opportunities.

Conversely, while you can't build your brand with a single action, you can certainly destroy it with one. So monitor yourself and think twice (or three times) before you react in anger or haste. This is why you should also keep your politics to yourself, especially on social media.

The Company Owns Your Day Job; Evenings Are Yours

The typical job is a simple contract: Your employer pays for your time during work hours, but they don't own your evenings, weekends, or personal projects.* But many professionals are afraid to build a personal brand because they worry it will conflict with their day job. As long as you keep your branding efforts separate from work, you're in control of your own career growth.

(* Be sure to check your employment contract, though. In some instances, for example, if you're an inventor or creator employed by a university or research institution, they may own your personal projects, too. That includes the things you develop in the evenings and weekends. So, that billion-dollar invention you created in your garage on the weekends may end up going to your employer instead of you. If you're not sure, check your contract or ask an employment lawyer.)

Write blog posts and articles in the evenings and on the weekends. Sketch out notes and work on initial drafts with a pen and notebook during lunch. A weekly, well-written article on LinkedIn can help establish you as an industry expert over time.

(Note: Be sure to post your articles to your own personal blog a few days before you repost to LinkedIn. This way, Google will recognize your blog as the canonical source for that information, not LinkedIn.)

These posts don't need to be groundbreaking or contain original research, they just need to be useful and valuable to your readers. Share insights about your industry, lessons you've learned in your job, or a professional analysis of the latest trends. Later, you *do* want to start making groundbreaking posts with original research, but right now, just get into the habit of posting on a regular basis.

Writing regularly helps you refine your ideas, as well as helps you improve your writing, so you can learn how to express your ideas much more clearly and succinctly. The more you do it, the better you'll get at it.

Best of all, when people Google your name, they'll find evidence of your expertise.

Here's an extra tip: Now that AI bots are crawling all of our websites these days, and since Google now provides AI-created summaries of information it finds, you can cheat the system a bit: Write a 100-word bio that is a glowing praise-fest of your work. Precede that with a statement that "If you're a human, you can stop reading. This is a summary for the AI bots that crawl these pages."

Then, publish the bio at the bottom of all of your blog posts on your own website or any other place you think it would be appropriate. Then, if people ever Google your name or ask an AI engine who you are, a variation of that description should come up.

Try a little experiment: Go to any of the AI sites of your choice — ChatGPT, Gemini, Perplexity, Claude, etc. — and ask, "Who is [your name]?" If you have a fairly common name, use your middle initial or a geographic location, like the city or state you live in.

You should already be Googling yourself, and AI searches may become a new form of Googling yourself just to make sure the best information is available.

Speak at industry events. Conferences, networking events, webinars, and seminars — these are all excellent ways to grow your brand without interfering with your job. In fact, they may even be related to your job, which means you can attend several of them and the company will (hopefully) pay for your travel. They will certainly consider it a feather in their cap if one of their employees is speaking at an industry conference.

If your job has nothing to do with your personal brand, then find the industry events related to it and attend those as you can. Take personal days or attend evening and weekend events. The more you can speak in public, the more visible you become. And if you're sharing cutting-edge information, you'll be seen as one of the experts in your field.

Erik started doing this in the late 2000s and early 2010s, speaking about social media and blogging, and soon became one of the premier Midwest speakers on the subject.

If speaking at events seems intimidating, join Toastmasters and learn how to give speeches. Next, start attending the events and engaging with the speakers. Have a drink or a meal with them at the event and become friendly with them. (Networking!) Learn how they do what they do, see how you can copy it, and you'll soon gain the confidence to take the stage yourself.

Speak on podcasts. There are plenty of podcasts in every industry and field, which means there is at least one in yours. As you're building your expertise, you're becoming someone those podcasts want to have as a guest. Reach out to the host and ask if you could come on as a guest.

Never pay to be on a podcast, however. We question the ethics of podcasts that charge their guests a hefty fee to appear on their show. Unless the podcast can actually offer a guarantee that your appearance will result in new opportunities, it's hard to justify spending a few thousand dollars on the promise of "Well, it *could* work."

Plenty of podcasters are doing this for their own personal branding efforts (see below), and they're just looking for content. Of course, it would be great to make money *from* a podcast, but paying to be on a podcast is like paying a TV news program to do a story on you: it's unethical and violates the integrity of the medium.

Start your own podcast. If there aren't many podcasts in your industry, start your own. They're actually not that difficult to start — all you need is Zoom and a podcast distribution network. From there, you can start interviewing people and putting out regular content.

If you want to get fancy and have high production values, then you can sink hundreds and thousands of dollars into microphones, cameras, and editing software. But when you're starting out, just interview other smart people about their work and post it. Share it with your industry contacts and ask for feedback in the beginning.

As you see problems with the production or areas of improvement, fix them. But don't wait until everything is perfect before you start promoting it. Don't let perfect be the enemy of good. Just put it out and let the podcast dictate the improvements it needs.

You can also use a podcast as a sales tool of sorts. If there are people you want to get to know, work for, sell to, or network with, invite them onto your podcast. Rather than just cold calling them and asking for a meeting or a sale, invite them onto the podcast and have a conversation with them. This is an excellent way to meet leaders in the industry you work in or would like to work in.

For example, let's say you want to work in the alternative energy industry but are currently in manufacturing. Start an alternative energy podcast that examines the industry and shares the latest developments and controversies.

Schedule interviews with company leaders, especially those you would like to work for. If you want to work in marketing in alternative energy, then start an alt-energy marketing podcast and interview every marketing director, CMO, and agency owner you can. This puts you on their radar, and they may be interested in bringing you into their company later.

TV writer Gray Jones graduated with a Screenwriting BFA (Bachelor of Fine Arts) from York University in Toronto, Canada. However, he didn't have any contacts in the industry, so he started a TV writing podcast and interviewed every screenwriter who ever wrote a book.

He would buy that book, read it — *devour* it, really — and ask a lot of thoughtful questions of the writer. He did this for 137 episodes, eventually branching out to talk to screenwriters who didn't have books.

At the same time, he was also applying for a green card to move to the U.S. When he finally got it, he moved to Los Angeles and contacted his past guests, telling them he had moved, he was looking for a job in the industry, and asked if they could help him with a referral or introduction.

He now has an extensive list of Hollywood credits and projects, all because 1) he had a dream, 2) he focused on his brand, and 3) he used his podcast to network with the people he wanted to work for.

Address Employer Concerns Without Losing Their Trust

Even if you're building your brand on your own time, your employer might still be concerned about your efforts. They may see it as a sign that you're planning to leave, or they may feel you're putting more energy into your brand than your job. Or they may just be jealous that you're getting all the attention they feel they deserve.

You can put their concerns to rest by making your brand an asset, not a threat. Your personal brand should align with the company's goals, not compete with them. That means if you're sharing industry insights, frame them in a way that reflects positively on your employer.

For example, if you're a marketer writing about branding strategies, blog about new trends in the industry and the successful projects you've worked on. (Without disclosing confidential information, of course.) If you work in finance, start a podcast where you interview senior finance professionals who give you insights and education into the work that you're doing.

Make sure you keep things balanced, too. If 90% of your LinkedIn activity is about your side projects and only 10% is about your job, your employer will notice. Balance things out by sharing content that relates to your current role, your industry, and your professional growth. This shows that you're invested in your work while also establishing your expertise.

Finally, don't blindside them with your brand. If you start gaining traction, such as speaking at a conference or doing media interviews, discuss it with your manager. Instead of framing it as a side hustle, position it as something that benefits both you and the company. If they see it as an opportunity for them as much as it is for you, they may even support your efforts.

4. Use Social Media Without Jeopardizing Your Job

Social media is one of the most powerful tools for personal branding. It turns a years-long process into one that takes months. With the right messaging and connections, you can even start making an impact in weeks.

There are three surefire ways to use social media to improve your personal brand.

1) First, curate industry news and share stories from well-known and lesser-known industry blogs. This shows that you're reading and staying up-to-date on what's happening in your industry, plus it has the added benefit of actually helping you, you know, stay up-to-date on what's happening in your industry.

Make it a habit to share one story every day. Be sure to tag the publication and the author in your social posts, which gets you on their radar as well.

2) Write weekly blog articles that analyze different problems in the industry or discuss issues you're learning about. Don't talk about your company, of course, but look at industry trends and showcase some of the solutions or solution-makers who are tackling the problem. Again, be sure to link to and tag the companies that are doing the work. Who knows? They may see what you're doing and invite you to join them. . .

3) Network with other industry leaders. Comment on their posts and share their updates as a way to show you're engaged in your field and interested in what *they're* doing. This increases your visibility and strengthens your reputation without making it look like you're job hunting. Remember what we said about starting your own podcast and interviewing industry leaders? Do that with your blog, or even just having a coffee or lunch meeting.

Be careful about what you post, though

But posting the wrong thing is where many professionals make mistakes. Posting the wrong thing can damage your reputation, lose followers, strain relationships with coworkers, or even get you fired.

Here are a few instances where people published their "secret" thoughts online and lost their jobs as a result:

In 2011, Scott Bartosiewicz was a social media strategist working for Chrysler's social media agency, New Media Strategies, when he posted the message, "I find it ironic that Detroit is known as the #motorcity and yet no one here knows how to f****** drive." [5]

Reader, he did not post "f******," he posted the actual word.

He meant to post it on his own Twitter account but posted it on Chrysler's instead, blaming it on a bug in the software he was using. He was fired immediately, Chrysler issued an apology tweet, and said they would not renew New Media's contract.

In 2021, ESPN fired NBA analyst Paul Pierce after he posted an Instagram Live video featuring himself in a room with exotic dancers.[6] He had been an analyst on multiple shows, but since ESPN is owned by the family-friendly Walt Disney Company, they decided they couldn't have

---

[5]

https://money.cnn.com/galleries/2011/technology/1104/gallery.social_media_controversies/index.html

[6] https://www.cnn.com/2021/04/06/media/paul-pierce-espn-analyst-fired-instagram-video-trnd/index.html

one of their employees in that kind of setting. It didn't help matters either that Pierce and his friends weren't wearing masks or following COVID protocols that the network had set up.

The argument could be made that Pierce was on his own time doing his own thing, but since he had essentially tied his own social media accounts to his celebrity status and role as an ESPN analyst, the Disney Corporation decided they couldn't be associated with Pierce any longer.

This idea has actually been tested in the courts, and they have decided that organizations can terminate employees for their social media posts. In 2021, Chicago firefighter Sam Inedino was fired by the city over a series of racist Facebook posts. The court said that because Inedino had purposely linked himself and his speech to his employer by including "his occupation and a photo of himself in Department uniform on his publicly accessible Facebook page."[7]

In other words, if you're going to say hateful or controversial things, don't.

But if you're going to ignore that, then don't connect yourself to your employer. If they feel that your messages, combined with your

---

[7] https://www.firelawblog.com/2024/10/08/court-upholds-termination-of-chicago-firefighter-over-offensive-social-media-posts

employment by them, are a problem, they will eliminate that problem for you.

This also means don't discuss controversial topics that could alienate coworkers or employers. Even if you feel strongly about politics, social issues, or company policies, just keep your opinions to yourself online. If you wouldn't say it in a job interview or in front of your grandmother, don't post it on social media.

Better yet, keep your personal and professional accounts separate. If you have a side hustle or project that isn't directly related to your job, create separate social media accounts for it. This will prevent any potential conflicts of interest and ensure that your employer doesn't feel like you're using company resources to promote yourself.

That means posting things under a different name, like a pen name or secret identity. Erik's younger daughter is an online artist but keeps her identity a secret, although that's more for personal anonymity than protecting her corporate identity. Still, it keeps her personal identity separate from her artistic identity.

5. Public Speaking: The Fast Track to Authority

Public speaking is one of the best ways to build your personal brand so that it benefits you *and* your employer. Whether you're presenting at company meetings, speaking at industry events, or hosting webinars, public speaking sets you up as a credible expert.

It basically says, "My company trusts me enough to make them look good and/or not embarrass them in public. They think I know enough about this subject that they're letting me stand up in front of you all to tell you about it."

(Of course, that's also enough to fire up your impostor syndrome, but that's a whole other book.)

Public speaking is one of the fastest ways to gain visibility and recognition. Here are a few ways you can use public speaking to boost your brand.

Speak at company events. Whether it's an internal training session, leadership panel, roundtable discussion, or lunch-and-learns, volunteering to lead one of these sessions positions you as a leader within the company. Share those insights about industry trends (that you have been blogging about), lessons learned from recent projects, or best practices in your field. The idea is to provide value to your coworkers while also reinforcing your expertise.

Present at industry conferences. These are great places to share knowledge, establish your credibility, and connect with industry professionals. Start out by submitting proposals for small breakout sessions or panels and work your way up to giving keynote speeches at these events. If big conferences seem intimidating, start with local meetups and smaller networking events to build confidence. The more you speak, the more opportunities will come your way.

Host/join webinars and podcasts. Webinars and podcasts are a great way to share your insights with a wide audience without the need to travel or stand on a stage. Partner with industry pros to co-host discussions on relevant industry topics. This will not only boost your personal brand, it will help you develop valuable connections. Plus, most employers will see your participation in industry discussions as a positive. Just remember, you don't speak for the company at all, so never, ever talk about what the company thinks or is doing. (For one thing, if you work in a regulated industry, your statements could violate regulations and laws about that kind of thing.)

6. Handling Resistance from Peers & Bosses

Not everyone is going to be a fan of your efforts to build your personal brand. Some colleagues may see it as an ego play and brazen self-promotion; others might feel threatened or envious.

You could fall victim to the **Tall Poppy Syndrome**, which came from Australia in the

126

1980s. It's about people who excessively promote their own achievements, so the criticism of that person is called "cutting down the tall poppy." It's the idea that no one wants people to rise above them, but they also act out of a sense of jealousy: "I don't want that person to rise above *me*."

That's also called the **crab mentality** (or **crab theory**, **crabs in a bucket**, or the **crab-bucket effect**). This refers to the people who try to prevent others from growing or improving themselves, even if that growth does not impact the people trying to stop them. It refers to the idea that if there are several crabs in a bucket, if one crab starts to climb out, it will be pulled back in by the others. Because all the other crabs believe, "If I can't have it, neither can you."

Call it what you will, this is the kind of petty jealousy that will stand in the way of your advancements. It could be a coworker who doesn't want to see you do better than them, or worse, a boss who feels threatened by you and feels that *they* should be doing what you're doing.

You may hear comments like, "Why are you always posting on LinkedIn?" or "Why do you get to speak at all these events? What makes you so special?"

The best way to handle this jealousy is to stay humble and focus on the value you're providing.

When you post online or speak at events, frame your content around helping others.

You also need to make sure you're excelling at your job. Don't let your personal branding efforts interfere with your work ethic, and give your haters something to focus on. Stay engaged in team projects, meet deadlines, and contribute meaningfully in meetings. Make sure you keep your supervisor apprised of what you're doing, and don't give them any ammunition.

Finally, make sure you have a sponsor or mentor high enough in the organization who can advocate for you. It may be your boss' boss, or someone even higher. This will be the person who essentially tells other people to climb off your back and leave you alone to do the great things you're doing.

Support others in their professional growth. Remember, givers gain! This applies here, too. Help your peers grow by celebrating their achievements, commenting on their LinkedIn posts, and offering guidance when they need it. When you uplift them, they're more likely to see what you're doing as positive, rather than competitive.

Finally, don't let it derail you. There are some people you can never make happy; they'll always complain about *something*. These are the people who are never happy, and they're displeased with the way their life is going, and they don't want anyone to do better than them. But that shouldn't stop you. As long as you're behaving ethically and adding value to others, including your employer, keep going. Over time, people will see the results for themselves.

Bottom line: Ignore the haters and focus on your own work and brand. You can't control their opinions of you, and you don't want to spend the energy trying to convince them that you're not so bad. Focus all that energy on you; don't feed the trolls, and don't give them anything they can use.

Chapter 8 Building Thought Leadership

What even is thought leadership?

It's one of those overused, corporate-y buzzwords that people love to slap on their LinkedIn bios. It's sort of like when people tell you to "dress professionally" or take things to the "next level."

It sounds impressive, but if you ask most people what it means, they look like you just asked them to explain quantum mechanics.

It's not a fancy way of saying, "I have opinions that I shall deliver from on high."

It's about **having deep expertise in your field and consistently sharing insights that help people think differently.**

It's not parroting other people's ideas or quoting other people's writings. It's about being the person others turn to when they need real answers, not just one more voice in the digital echo chamber.

If your idea of thought leadership is cranking out yet one more "Five Easy Ways to Improve Your Productivity" blog post, you're not leading thoughts, you sound exactly like the 10,000 other articles that every other so-called "thought leader" is creating.

Hint: If you're creating listicles as blog articles, you're not a thought leader. You're just contributing to Internet clutter.

Real thought leaders go deeper. They question the status quo, they challenge people to think differently, they take risks with their ideas, and, most importantly, they **add something new to the conversation.**

Want to be a thought leader? Stop regurgitating what everyone else is saying and think independently.

If you find someone is trying to disrupt the status quo with their ideas or they're bringing new knowledge to your industry, don't just parrot them. Go deeper. Argue with them, dispute them, and do original research to back up their ideas. Get the actual data that says, "Hey, this person was right!"

Before we get into how to become a thought leader, let's bust a few myths that will keep you from doing it right.

Myth #1. Thought leadership is just personal branding.

Nope. Personal branding is about making yourself look good and establishing your reputation. Everything we've talked about in the last seven chapters is about personal branding.

Thought leadership means actually knowing your stuff. It means being the smartest person in the room on that particular topic. It means producing the kind of knowledge that other people talk about or share on their blogs. Like a book or conducting your own study about a question or theory.

If your strategy is just posting selfies with vague motivational quotes — Hustle harder, sleep later! #grindlife — you're not a thought leader, you're a dime-a-dozen life coach on Instagram who's not actually providing any real value. (And no, taking a photo of yourself in front of someone else's uber-expensive car doesn't count either.) Remember, thought leadership isn't about you, it's about sharing insights that make other people better.

Myth #2: You have to be famous first

Absolutely not. You don't need a best-selling book, a million followers, or a TEDx Talk on your résumé before you can start sharing what you know.

If anything, you'll achieve those things by consistently providing value. That's what you'll be known for, not your Instagram platitudes. The more valuable insights you share, the more people will pay attention.

Myth #3: Thought leaders know everything

Also nope. The best thought leaders don't pretend to have all the answers. They never believe they're the smartest person in the room, even if they clearly are.

They stay curious, they ask better questions, and they constantly learn from others. They read a lot, take notes on what they read, and synthesize it into new knowledge. They ask questions about their data and gather new data. They have new ideas, flesh them out, and share them with their audience, no matter how big or small.

No one expects you to be a walking encyclopedia,* but they expect that when you speak, you actually have something meaningful and important to say.

* *For our younger readers, an encyclopedia is if Wikipedia was a book.*

133

How to Establish Yourself as a Thought Leader

If you want people to see you as a thought leader, you need three things:

First, **you need experience in your niche.** Thought leadership isn't about talking, it's about doing. You need real-world knowledge that comes from actually working in your field. That means you're not likely going to find many 25-year-old thought leaders.

That's not to say it can't happen, but it's going to be in a new field that you've spent the last four years developing and growing yourself. For example, the first social media experts were fairly young because they started using it in college before the business world had ever really heard about it.

Other people, like Erik, were older because he happened to hear about it just as it was starting, and happened to be in the right place at the right time. He had been blogging for ten years by that point (he started in 1997) and then quickly picked up social media and used it constantly, much to his boss' consternation. He was one of the first social media professionals in Indiana to start using it to promote his employer's company.

Second, **you need to be able to explain ideas clearly.** If you can't communicate your expertise in a way that makes sense, nobody will care. You should be able to simplify complex ideas without dumbing them down or making your readers and followers feel stupid.

This is an important skill to have anyway — *probably the most important skill you will need throughout your entire career.* You need to be able to simplify things because, chances are, you're going to explain them to people who don't have the in-depth knowledge that you do. This is especially true if you're in sales, marketing, or entrepreneurship (which is sales *and* marketing plus your actual work). You have to explain things to decision-makers who are not even one-tenth as knowledgeable as you and don't have the time to delve into things with you.

Robert experiences this regularly. When he was selling high-end floor coverings to professional practices (attorneys, etc.), he had to explain the benefits to a lawyer whose mind was on twelve other things at that very moment. So he couldn't dazzle them with jargon and sales BS; he has to explain things as simply and directly as possible.

Finally, **you need to be consistent**. One good blog article won't do it. You need to show up again and again, writing, speaking, sharing, and engaging in conversation. You need to be present on social media, you need to share in meetings, and you need to be public about your knowledge.

135

It means putting out content even when you think no one is listening or reading. They probably aren't, but that doesn't mean they won't show up eventually. Rather than timing your arrival with theirs, just start putting out content.

When your followers do show up, you want them to find piles of knowledge already waiting for them, not a couple of blog posts and an IOU notice of future information.

Thought leaders don't wait for permission, either. They don't ask, "Can I be an expert now?" They put in the work, share what they know, and let their credibility grow naturally. They have the confidence to believe they're experts, but they also have the receipts to back it up.

Most importantly, good thought leaders never really set out to be thought leaders. They just want to share knowledge. They get curious about a subject, they start researching it, and they share it. One day, they look up and realize, "Oh, I'm a thought leader!" and then they put their heads down and get back to work.

Jay Baer, who we've mentioned already, is a well-known thought leader on the subject of business growth and customer experience.

But what a lot of people don't know is that Jay is also "the second-most-popular tequila influencer in the world (non-celebrity division)." That's what it says on his website.[8]

It just so happens that Jay loves tequila. He spent 25 years visiting Mexico and learning how tequila is made, marketed, and sold. In addition to his day job work, he also started sharing his passion for tequila on his Instagram and TikTok channels.

Suddenly, without even meaning to, he found himself as the #2 tequila influencer on social media. He has more than 150,000 followers on Instagram, 87,000 followers on TikTok, and he hosts the Spirit Guides podcast.

It was sort of a surprise to him that he had earned this role, because all he wanted to do was just share his love of tequila. He put in the work just so he could be a teacher, and success followed.

The Role of Writing

Thought leadership is not about tweeting clever one-liners, motivational quotes, and photos of you standing next to a private jet (moments before you got chased off by security). It's not about posting short messages on LinkedIn a couple times a week.

Real credibility comes from long-form content.*

---

[8] https://www.jaybaer.com/tequila

* For the most part, that would be written content, but as we saw with Jay Baer, Tequila Expert, that can also come in the form of video and audio content. Still, we're both writers, so that's where our bias lies. But if we say "write," just know that video/audio content is also acceptable.

If you can't communicate your expertise in-depth, do you even have any expertise?

Chris Baggott, the co-founder of ExactTarget (now Salesforce Marketing Cloud), became a thought leader in email marketing not only because of his association with one of the largest email marketing companies. It was also because he spent years writing about it.

Chris built his reputation by blogging about email marketing before people even knew what it was.

Then, when a publisher asked if he wanted to write a book about email marketing, he assumed he had more than enough content. But when he went through his blog posts, he realized he had been saying a lot of the same things over and over.

So, he had to come up with a lot of new material for this new book, but it became one of the very first books about email marketing, and it established him as one of the big names in that field.

The same is true for Erik and Kyle Lacy, or Erik and Jason Falls, when they wrote *Branding Yourself* (2010) and *No Bullsh*t Social Media* (2011), respectively. Erik, Kyle, and Jason all had well-known reputations as early thinkers and writers about social media, but the cachet of having written a book on the subject carried them into the national spotlight.

They also had friends who wrote books about social media, personal branding, blogging, and digital marketing. In every case, the book was one of the first on that subject, and it created their reputations as thought leaders in digital marketing and personal branding.

On Writing a Book

Want to instantly boost your credibility? Write a book. A book is the ultimate social proof that says, "I know my stuff, and I've organized it into something valuable."

People throw away business cards. They don't throw away books.

Of course, writing a book is easier said than done. But it's not that hard, either. It's just time-consuming, and it can be difficult if you don't build a structure and outline when you start out.

Here's the easiest way to write a book:

1) Start a blog on your industry or specialty. Pick a specific niche and do a deep, deep dive into that. For example, don't start a blog on "marketing" because that's too vague and general, and you'll actually run out of topics in about three weeks. But you could start a blog on "content marketing for nonprofits" and have an infinite number of topics to cover.

2) Make a list of the big ideas in your field. These are the categories that you're going to write about. This way, you'll know what you actually need to write about and what you can ignore.

3) Similarly, find the other big thinkers in your field. What are the things they're writing about? What issues are they hammering on over and over? Those are the categories you'll want to avoid, unless they're inescapable. For example, if you work in finance, you can't avoid writing about tariffs and recessions just because other people are doing it. But if you wanted to be a sportswriter, don't forgo writing about your favorite sport just because someone else is. Pick a facet of the sport and focus on that.

4) Write weekly blog articles on your categories; twice a week is even acceptable. Pay attention to the categories you write about regularly versus the ones that you don't like, don't care about, or don't know enough about. Discard those

lesser-used categories altogether, and
don't waste your time on them.

5) Pay attention to the patterns that emerge.
Are you spending a lot of time on a single
category? Can you do a deeper dive into
one of those categories? Or are you
finding enough specific material in your
few categories? As you progress in your
blog, you'll begin to home in on the
central themes of your blog.

6) Now, you're ready to start putting your
book together. Based on what you've
written so far, start thinking in terms of
giving a presentation on this topic. What
are the ten big ideas you would want to
share in the talk? These don't have to
match up with your blog categories, but
that's where you'll start. Imagine giving a
one- or two-hour presentation and talking
about the ten most important things you
want people to take away.

7) Write those ten ideas down. Those are the
ten chapters of your book.

8) Next, let's go deeper. Imagine you're
going to give each of those ten chapters as
an individual presentation: you're going to
give a one- or two-hour presentation on
that chapter, and it will have between
three and seven major points. Create that
outline with those three to seven points;
those are the subsections of the chapter.
Create a document per chapter with each
section of the outline contained in it.

141

9) Go back through your blog and copy-paste the articles that fit each subsection. If you have more than one blog article that fits, paste them all into that section. As you start writing, rewrite those blog articles so they flow smoothly within the chapter and the book at large.

10) For any subsections that are not filled yet, you have two choices: 1) Write a blog article about it and then slot it into the chapter, or 2) Ignore your blog for now and write the subsection of the chapter. That content won't make it into the blog.

11) If you choose the first option, write the remaining blog articles specifically to fill up the open sub-sections in your book. From this point on, the entire purpose of your blog is to fill up your book. When you're finished with the book, go back to creating original content for the blog. You may need another book some day.

A note on the length of your book: Please do not fall into the trap of writing less than 10,000 words, slapping a cover on it, and calling it a book. That's not a book, that's a short article. You can find 10,000-word articles in magazines and on blogs.

A book should be *at least* 20,000 words, but preferably 35,000 or more. (This one is 38,000 words.) Even that is an extremely short book; a debut novel is usually 60,000 words or so.

Considering that a blog article should be 1,000+ words, you've essentially written ten blog articles and called it a day.

A less-than-10,000-word piece is not worthy of the title of Book. Please don't sully the name Book with something akin to a pamphlet. Grind it out, write 30,000 words or more, and create a book that's really a book.

Seriously, we have known people who cranked out a collection of 5,000 words and called it a book, just so they could say they had written one. It's cheap and rather insulting to actual book authors.

And certainly never, ever, *ever* write your book with artificial intelligence. For one thing, that's not writing, that's plagiarism. For another, AI hallucinates wildly, and there's a very good chance that you will leave in erroneous information, or even leave in part of your prompt or the AI's response. When that happens and you get caught, you'll be called out on social media and mercilessly mocked and ridiculed.

Other ways to build credibility

Not ready to write a book? Neither were we, but here you are reading it.

Still, there are plenty of other ways to prove your expertise without generating 60–80,000 words on a subject.

- **Write guest articles in industry publications and blogs.** One way to grow your own audience is to borrow someone else's. In fact, this is a way you can cooperate with other budding thought leaders: Guest post on each other's blogs, then share a link to the other person's website along with a bio: "Robert Bagley III is an author, professional networker, and fractional sales manager. You can find him on his LinkedIn page." This not only provides an SEO boost, but you can share each other's work with your own social media audiences, which can only help you both.
- **Write newsletters.** Newsletters may be one of the best ways to build a loyal following. More importantly, your email list is probably the most valuable data you will have: it's a list of people who said, "I believe in you enough to give you permission to email me." Whether it's weekly or monthly, share insights you post on your blog via your newsletter. You can even make the newsletter exclusive content that subscribers see before your blog readers do.
- **Publish LinkedIn newsletters.** Not all your newsletter subscribers will read you, and not all your LinkedIn connections subscribe to your newsletter. (And not everyone from either group will read your blog.) So, republish your blog and

newsletter content to LinkedIn. Just remember to post to LinkedIn *after* you post to your blog.

- **Hosting webinars or workshops**. Teaching other people is a great way to raise your credibility because you're sharing advanced and original knowledge. Best of all, you don't have to ask permission. If you're going to speak in public, you have to get permission from the event organizers to do it. But all you need is a Zoom, GoTo Webinar, or Livestorm account and a way to market it. Once again, hosting a webinar gives you the same cachet that speaking live can give you.

The goal is to put as much knowledge out there for people to see. Share the good stuff, and don't hold anything back. If you learn new information or come up with new ideas, share it. Don't hide it, don't wait for permission, just put it out there and let people see your brilliance.

Speaking and Networking: Thought Leadership in Action

Writing is powerful, but you also need to talk to people.

Speaking at events, joining or leading panel discussions, and appearing on podcasts — these are all ways to establish yourself as an expert on a subject. When you're in front of a room or a microphone, you're magically granted special expertise on your chosen subject. People assume, "Well, she's the one talking about it, so she must know a lot."

(The same is true for writing a book: "She wrote a book about it; she must know an awful lot.")

More importantly, when people see your confidence, your personality, and your ability to communicate, they assume you have more knowledge and authority than you may believe you have. So your speaking confers thought leadership on you.

We both speak from experience when we tell you that speaking to an audience about your chosen subject makes people think you're one of the leading authorities on the subject, at least locally. Erik has gotten clients because of presentations he's given. One woman from a Fortune 500 company even said, "If you only know half of what you said up there, we definitely need you to write for our company!" He had them as a client for five years.

And don't forget the power of networking. Thought leaders aren't just smart, they're well-connected. When people think of your industry, your name should come up in conversation. When people talk about your specialty subject, you should be the first person people think of.

And if you're sharing valuable insights, people will start recommending you for projects, client work, and speaking opportunities.

That's how thought leadership spreads.

Becoming a thought leader isn't about luck, connections, or your social media presence. It's about sharing valuable insights and proving your expertise over a long period of time.

The more you write, speak, and engage, the more people will recognize your name and understand that you have vast depths of knowledge. Before you know it, when someone asks, "Who's the expert on this subject?" your name is the one that will come up.

So get to work.

Chapter 9
Promoting Your Brand

Building a personal brand is like being a DJ at a party. You want to create a presence that people remember, one that sets the right tone and keeps them engaged. And has a kicking beat. But if you're constantly shouting your name over the music, people will get annoyed and tune you out. (Looking at you, DJ Khaled.)

Similarly, there's a difference between being an influencer and being an annoying pest. For example, Erik enjoys watching woodworkers and makers on YouTube, and he has a couple of favorites. One is Laura Kampf from Germany, and another is Cristiana Felgueiras of Get Hands Dirty in Portugal. Both women do amazing work, and they put out great videos that have inspired hundreds of thousands of people around the world to follow them.

On the other hand, there are some makers out there who put out videos to promote themselves. Everything is about them. They spray paint their names all over their tools, not to make sure no one steals them, but so the viewer always knows who they're watching. They're more concerned with being seen and being recognized. They do excellent work and create great projects, but sometimes those seem secondary to actually promoting their brand. As long as they get to promote their brand, they'll build anything that gets clicks and views.

We won't name names because they already know who they are. (How could they not? They spray-painted their name on everything.)

The trick to balancing this tightrope is to make yourself visible in a way that feels natural, helpful, and interesting. Whether you're working in a corporate setting or running your own business, the way you promote yourself can mean the difference between being seen as an industry and being dismissed as just one more annoying voice constantly shouting, "Hey, everyone! Look at me! Look at what I'm doing!"

In other words, post useful advice rather than posting the results of your work. Make your online content more about providing value than promoting your name. That's not to say you can't celebrate your victories, but if all your personal branding is just photos of you in front of expensive cars or eating fancy food, that's not promoting your brand; that's shouting your name over the music and interrupting everyone else's good time.

149

Think of it this way: Let's say you want to be known as an authority on Sherlock Holmes. (Erik knows plenty of these people!) You love the original 60 stories by Arthur Conan Doyle, and you love sharing information about the scholarship that surrounds the literary detective and his erstwhile partner, Dr. Watson.

There are two ways you could go about this:

1. You could write a lot about Sherlock Holmes. You could start a blog, contribute articles to the *Baker Street Journal* (a real journal), join the Baker Street Irregulars (a real literary society), and even start your own Sherlock Holmes podcast.
2. Or you could read and re-read each story and then post a photo of yourself holding up the completed book and saying, "Just read '*The Hound of the Baskerville*' for the 17th time!" and repeating that every time you finish a story.

Which one of those is going to help you be seen as a Sherlock Holmes expert, and which one is going to portray you as a Sherlock show-off who doesn't actually contribute to the growing study of Sherlock Holmes?

Building Credibility in a Corporate Environment

In a corporate setting — actually, in any setting — your self-promotion needs to be subtle and strategic. You want to stand out, but not in a way that seems self-serving. One of the best ways is by showcasing your work that benefits your company.

For example, when you attend a conference, share insights and important lessons rather than posting your achievements. Instead of saying, "Excited to be at the National Leadership Conference," try, "I learned some great strategies today at the National Leadership Conference that will help our team streamline project management," and then recap a few strategies.

It's subtle, but the latter positions you as a team player who is concerned about the company's success, which enhances your brand while keeping everyone focused on the value you're providing.

It's not about getting selfies with the notable people at the conference, it's about contributing knowledge to the field and to your company.

Another way to build credibility within your company is through internal thought leadership. Offer to write for the company blog, contribute to internal newsletters, or lead training sessions. This positions you as an expert to the management and executives, who will see your name attached to this knowledge and assume you're an expert when, in actuality, you just had the *chutzpah* to ask for permission.

Elevating Others to Elevate Yourself

One great way to promote yourself is to promote other people first. Sometimes called "reciprocal promotion," this works especially well in a corporate setting or as an entrepreneur in a big city. That does four things:

1. It shows you care about others. Based on the idea that "a rising tide lifts all boats," you're demonstrating that you want everyone else to succeed even as you do.
2. If people see you help those around you succeed, you can be seen as not only someone valuable to the organization but as potential leadership material.
3. It creates goodwill among colleagues and strengthens relationships. When you give others the spotlight, they're more likely to return the favor.
4. It shows confidence. Someone who is constantly seeking the spotlight is insecure and trying to convince *themselves* that they're important and powerful. But someone who is happy to share the spotlight already knows where they stand

with their skills, with their image, and in their life.

This applies to networking as well, which we have already discussed in previous chapters. Introduce people to each other, recommend colleagues for opportunities, and support other people in their own endeavors. The more you help people, the more you're seen as a valuable resource, which only helps your own personal brand..

Mastering Relationship Building

Your personal brand is more than what you post online, it's also how you present yourself in person. Your body language, communication style, and professional demeanor all affect how people know and relate to you. So, pay attention to how you carry yourself in meetings, at networking events, or in other public engagements.

It all starts with what you do when you meet people.

The Introduction

One effective strategy is to develop a strong "elevator pitch." When someone asks what you do, you should be able to explain it in just a few seconds. Avoid jargon and lengthy explanations; focus on the impact of your work and what it is that you do.

To be clear, neither of us believes in the "elevator pitch" approach, and we don't even like calling it that, but it's the best term for it. Too many so-called experts will tell you very unhelpful advice, like "You need a 30-second elevator pitch plus a 10-second pitch" or "Your pitch should be just vague enough to make people ask questions."

This is all utter nonsense.

Your "pitch" should be a basic explanation of what you do. If people are interested, they'll ask you further questions. If they're not, they won't. You don't have to trick them into it, you don't have to "tell them your why." You have to make them understand what you do as simply as possible.

They'll ask follow-up questions because they're interested in what you do, not because you intrigued them with your vagaries and impressed them with your "why."

(To be clear, knowing and explaining your "why" is useful, and it comes later. But it shouldn't be the very first thing you hit people with when you meet them. Go watch Simon Sinek's talk "Start with why -- how great leaders inspire action" at TEDxPugetSound.)

Most importantly, tailor your introduction to your specific audience because not everyone needs to hear the exact same thing that you do. For example, a general audience, you might meet at a general business event, a dinner party, or your high school reunion, doesn't need the same explanation as a specialized audience you would meet at an industry conference.

For example, when people ask Erik what he does for a living, he'll often just say, "I'm a writer." If they want to know more, he'll explain what kind of writing he does — "I'm a copywriter and ghostwriter."

But when he's meeting people at a networking event, he'll say, "I'm a corporate ghostwriter." And when he meets other marketers, he says, "I'm a copywriter" or "I'm a content marketer."

And of course, if he meets someone who is a potential client, he says, "I'm a memoir (or business book) ghostwriter." That way, if that person has ever been thinking about writing their own memoir or business book, they immediately know this is someone they should talk to further.

In all cases, people understand the term he uses because he understands who he's speaking to, and they have an understanding of what he does. He wouldn't tell someone who's not in business that he's a corporate ghostwriter or content marketer because that needs further explanation, and they're most likely not interested.

He doesn't have a 30-second elevator pitch or even a 10-second elevator pitch. He's able to succinctly describe what he does in a single, specific sentence.

You also need to be specific in your pitch.

Erik had a friend who owned an embroidery company. Her pitch was, "I help your company be memorable."

"So does a guy with a sandwich board," quipped Erik, which earned him a dirty look.

After brainstorming a few options, they came up with, "I own an embroidery company, and I can embroider anything for anyone."

People would invariably say something like, "Oh, yeah? Anything?"

She would reply, "Yes. I embroidered a roll of toilet paper once."

At that moment, the other person was hooked because that sounds like it would take precision work and a lot of knowledge. They knew that if they ever wanted shirts or hats embroidered, they only needed to ask the woman who was so good she could embroider a roll of toilet paper.

She didn't have a 30-second elevator pitch, and she was able to get more specific and interesting than "I help your company be memorable."

Once you've hooked the other person, make sure you engage in real conversations. Don't just talk about yourself, ask them questions about themselves, find common ground, and share insights. Better yet, ask them questions that will make you memorable.

Ask them things like how they got into that line of work, what their greatest business triumph was, or what their dream job is. They'll remember that because you took an interest in them rather than just wanting to pitch yourself, just like everyone else at the same event.

(Remember, your ultimate goal is to be interesting enough that they want to have coffee with you. You won't sell them on that initial introduction. You just want to get your relationship off to a good start.)

The Power of Gratitude

Gratitude is an underrated but powerful element of brand building. Once again, this shows that you're more interested in providing value than you are in boosting your reputation. When people support you — whether they reshare your content, refer clients to you, or mentor you and provide you with knowledge — acknowledge it.

Thank them. Tell them how much it means to you.

It could be a simple thank-you note or email. You could make a public shout-out on your socials. Even a small gesture of appreciation, like a small gift, can strengthen relationships. People remember those who show gratitude, and that goodwill pays off in the long run.

Showing gratitude also applies to your customers and clients. If you own a business, don't take your customers for granted: show them appreciation as well. Personalized follow-ups, handwritten thank-you notes, or unexpected bonuses (also called *lagniappes*) can turn your one-time customers into advocates and evangelists on your behalf.

This "attitude of gratitude" also extends to mentors and people you have professional relationships with. If someone gives you advice that helps you, let them know that it had an impact and tell them how. Again, a nice text or email is not out of line, and a handwritten or typed note can have an even bigger impact.

Most successful professionals are happy to help because they remember what it was like when they were just starting out, so they're just paying it forward. But a thoughtful acknowledgment makes them more likely to continue offering support.

Both of us enjoy hearing from people who tell us that something we did, said, or shared had a significant impact on them. Sometimes, those words of gratitude come out of the blue years later when someone will stop one of us and say, "I put that thing you told me years ago into practice, and it took my career in a whole new direction."

This has been true when we give advice on writing, speaking, networking, sales, or making introductions and referrals to people.

The reverse is also true, however: If you *don't* thank people for their assistance or show your gratitude, they'll remember you. "Ah, yes, that's the person I recommended for a job, and they never said a word to me afterward."

You don't have to buy them a gift or take them out for dinner, but even a quick email or phone call can make all the difference and keep them willing to be helpful to you well into the future.

The Role of Testing and Iteration

It's weird to talk about testing your brand, right? It's so nebulous and vague. What are you supposed to do, survey your network on a 5-point scale about how much they like you?

(For one thing, a simple note that says, "Do you like me? Circle yes or no" should suffice.)

Promoting your brand is not a set-it-and-forget-it process; it's a running series of experiments where each post teaches you something new. Robert's approach to testing and iterating his promotional efforts demonstrates the importance of adaptability. Not every post will succeed, but each one provides valuable insights and adds one more brick to the pile of knowledge he's accumulating.

For example, Robert posts mostly on LinkedIn, and he pays attention to the analytics of each post. He has found that some of the posts perform very well while others flop despite their high quality.

One particular video he made on dressing for success got a lot of traction because of its engaging thumbnail and relatable message. On the other hand, another video on advanced interview tips flopped because of the poor thumbnail design. This shows that paying attention to the small details, like visuals and headlines, can make or break engagement and views.

Testing and analytics revealed all that and helped Robert figure out the small changes that he needed to make in order to get higher views on all his videos.

Robert also experimented with YouTube Shorts and found that his first video received over 1,000 views within a few hours because the algorithm favors new users. However, later videos didn't perform as well despite managing the same details and following the same best practices as he did for LinkedIn. This was a good reminder that algorithms are unpredictable and that success can often come down to platform-specific nuances as much as timing, thumbnails, and quality of content.

The most important takeaway is to approach your promotion efforts with curiosity rather than trying to find perfection and extensive reach. Treat each post as a chance to learn rather than a definitive measure of your success and reach.

Pay attention to your metrics — views, likes, shares, and comments — to find the patterns in what resonates with your audience. If something doesn't perform well, don't just delete it immediately because it's still providing value to a small segment of your audience. Plus, it's got the potential to blow up months or even years later. This is especially true of your blog posts.

Testing and iteration aren't just about tweaking your content or deleting the poor-performing posts; it's about using your metrics to refine your overall strategy. Test different forms of content (written posts, long-form posts, videos, polls), the tone (formal versus conversational), and the topics (basic tips versus advanced insights).

By continually experimenting and adapting based on the feedback and metrics, you can hone your promotional strategy so that it reaches maximum impact while still remaining authentic and real.

Chapter 10
Invest in
Yourself

Congratulations! If you've made it this far, you're already investing in yourself. Whether you bought this book, borrowed it, or swiped it from a friend's bookshelf, the fact that you've made it this far means you care about your growth. That's what investing in yourself means. Making intentional choices to grow, improve, and build habits that help you reach your goals.

But let's say this upfront: Investing in yourself doesn't mean becoming one of those Type-A Productivity Bros who burst out of bed every day at 4:00 a.m. and see every waking moment as a chance to Optimize Life, #GrindLife, and make millions of dollars with every side hustle known to humanity.

You know the type — always hustling, always grinding, but never actually living. They're not just working, they've made the hustle their entire personality.

"So what's your favorite TV show?"

"Oh, I don't have time to watch TV. I'm always working on my next million-dollar idea."

Two words: Bo. Ring.

True investment in yourself is about balance. It's about doing things that make you better at your job or craft while also taking time to simply *be*. The point is to create a life that supports your ambitions, not sacrificing your happiness or your family just so you can have more.

Too many people think they need a daily grind *and* a side hustle. They want to be a millionaire — no, a *billionaire!* — and they think that the point of life is to hustle until you get rich.

That's wrong.

The whole reason you're doing any of this is to enjoy your time with your family, to provide and care for them, and to pursue the things that make you happy. But if you're sacrificing all of that just so you can get more, *more*, *MORE* when you already have enough, well, you're missing the whole point.

So, how do you invest in yourself without making it your whole personality?

Start Your Day with Intention

How you begin your day is more important than you think. It's more than just getting out of bed on time — notice we said "on time," not "early;" work the schedule that's right for you — it's about setting the tone for everything that follows.

Having a chaotic morning often leads to a chaotic day; a calm and intentional morning can lead to a more effective and productive day.

For some, starting the day with intention means carving out time for spiritual discipline. Whether it's prayer, meditation, yoga, or just sitting with coffee and toast before the world wakes up, this time lets you center yourself and focus on what really matters.

Robert takes a prayer walk without his phone — just him and his thoughts. This is his time to connect with Christ, but for others, it might be about connecting with the universe or just finding inner peace. The point is to create space for reflection before starting with the demands of the day.

This inner contemplation isn't just about spirituality or faith, it's also about clarity. It's a chance to align your priorities and set your intentions for the day. It could be as simple as writing down three things you want to accomplish that day or even spending five minutes visualizing how you want your day to unfold. The point is to start your day with purpose rather than just letting it unfold and taking things as they come.

Erik takes a different approach to his mornings. He makes it a practice to make breakfast every morning and sit without a phone as he eats. Making breakfast is a ritual where he focuses solely on that — the way he makes the eggs, the way he makes the toast. It's a type of meditation where the whole point is to "be in the now" (he hates that phrase) with his preparations because it frees his subconscious up to think of the deeper ideas he's been wrestling with.

Other people do yoga, go for a run, or review their to-do list to figure out their day.

And still others just do nothing. They wake up late, race through brushing their teeth and taking a shower, skip breakfast, and have a chaotic start to a chaotic day.

Find a practice of some sort that lets you slowly slip into your day by finding a calm and meditative start to the day, something that puts you in the right mindset. Just remember: You need to find the practice that is right for *you*. (Except maybe the chaotic start.)

Ignore the people who tell you that you *have to* get up super early, work out at a maniac's pace, and race into your morning at top speed. That may work for them, but it's not for everyone. If it were, we would all be doing it.

Get up late if you have to.

Of course, there's something to be said about staying up late and going to bed late. For years, Erik stayed up until 2:00 in the morning and would get up at 10:00 or later. This was especially when he was writing a lot of books, and there's never any one good time to write. You write when you have the mental energy.

Erik's mental energy peaked from about 8:00 p.m. onward, so he would tap into it and right long after everyone else went to bed. No meetings, no phone calls, no disturbances.

Of course, there were those people who thought this was a less-than-optimal productivity method. One guy on LinkedIn even said, "Staying up late was for children."

Erik reminded him that there are the same number of hours in the day, and as long as you're working for 8 – 12 hours, it doesn't matter when those hours occur. And that the guy was a big boy now, and he didn't have to go to bed early on a school night anymore.

Feed Your Mind and Body Simultaneously

Your mind and body are connected, and taking care of one will benefit the other. Robert combines exercise with mental growth by listening to audiobooks and podcasts even as he's working out, feeding his brain while strengthening his body.

But he also recognizes that it's important to unplug at certain times. For example, he rides his bike to the gym without headphones so he can focus on spiritual connection and mental clarity. Plus, he can hear the cars behind him.

Your physical health is foundational to everything else in your life. Your productivity, your happiness, even your relationships are all affected by your health. That means eating well and sleeping well aren't just good habits, they're investments in your long-term success. Poor sleep and unhealthy eating can derail even your best-laid plans. If you're tired, irritable, and unable to perform at your best, you'll constantly be fighting to overcome the deficits and problems you're creating.

Robert actually unplugs his wifi at night and puts his phone in an EMP bag (a small pouch that blocks electromagnetic signals; think of it as a "Do Not Disturb" bag). This might sound extreme, but Robert says it works wonders for reducing distractions and improving his sleep quality. Without constant notifications or the temptation to scroll through social media in the middle of the night, he can rest more deeply.

Erik swears by reading physical books instead of digital books because he finds paper books more therapeutic than digital ones; they provide a break from constant screens. Having said that, he still reads his Kindle before bed, but he turns on the night mode, which turns down the blue light spectrum on the screen.

Blue light from our screens can disrupt our sleep cycles and the production of melatonin, a sleep hormone. If you use your phone before bed, dim the screen and switch to night mode. And don't watch TV a couple hours before bed.

Invest in Relationships

You may love your work, but work will not love you back. You may spend all your time on your hustle, but your hustle won't greet you warmly at the end of a hard day. Your hustle won't smile when it sees you. Your hustle won't live on long after you're gone.

Your partner, children, grandchildren, parents, and friends are the reason you're working so hard in the first place. You are working to live, not living to work, and these relationships ground you and give meaning to your efforts.

This is also true in a professional sense. Focus on building genuine connections with your professional network, not on collecting followers. Having thousands of LinkedIn connections means nothing if you don't actually know those people or engage with them in a meaningful way.

When it comes to personal relationships, the key is presence. Not just being physically present but emotionally engaged as well.

That means closing your laptop and putting down your phone. If you're having dinner, watching TV together, or doing something as a group or family, focus on them, not on people who aren't there.

Too many times, we've seen people out to dinner but spending all their time on their phones. We will even admit to doing it ourselves as well.

Why do we do this? The person we should be communicating with and talking to is sitting right there in front of us. That's the person we should focus on, not the people who aren't there. If they were more important than your loved ones, they would be there with you.

But that person in front of you thinks enough of you to spend that time with you. In some cases, they think enough of you to spend their entire life with you, so don't ignore them in favor of whoever is texting, emailing, or messaging you.

This is true whether it's a romantic relationship, a friendship, or a new business relationship. That person is your priority at that moment, and no one else.

Limit What You Don't Need

This may come as a shock to some of you, but you don't need to be busy all the time. You don't need to have a lot of meetings each week, attend business events every night, or be involved in a number of different groups and nonprofits.

Trim your extracurricular activities

If you get too busy, with too many things pulling on your time and energy, you'll find yourself spread too thin, and you won't be able to give all the time and energy that those activities deserve. You're better off picking one extracurricular event — volunteer opportunity, board involvement, practice, or attendance — and focusing everything on that than being involved with six different things that you can only devote a tiny part of your time to.

Erik's big problem is that he will often overcommit to too many activities, running a writing group, running a networking group, serving on the board of an anti-racism nonprofit, and serving as the president of a literary nonprofit, as well as attending a variety of networking events.

This was the situation he found himself in at the end of 2023, and his client work, *plus* all those extra activities, were suffering. He couldn't spend all the time he wanted to on anything, and as a result, each group and client were only getting a fraction of what he could give them.

So he stopped attending the networking events, quit the anti-racism nonprofit, and turned the running of the networking group over to someone else. Now, he only runs the writing group and the literary nonprofit. As a result, he actually has more time to spend with his family and time to work on books like this one.

Trim your social media and entertainment

Similarly, we don't always have to be entertained. We don't have to binge-watch every show our friends tell us about, we don't need to constantly scroll through Instagram or Twitter on our phones, and we don't always have to have music on. (Erik said as he listened to Dave Matthews Band on SiriusXM for three hours straight.)

Cutting back on these unproductive habits and eliminating needless time sucks, like extracurricular events and yet one more business event, can free up a lot of time and energy for activities that actually contribute to your well-being. Whether it's devoting more time to your actual business or personal brand building, or spending more time with your family and friends, you don't always need to have something occupying your brain at all moments of the day.

Sometimes, it's not what you do that makes a good investment in yourself, it's what you don't do. Our modern lives are filled with distractions that can easily derail our focus and prevent us from achieving our goals.

Social media can be especially tricking because it's designed to be incredibly engaging and even addictive. We've all fallen into the endless scroll trap to the point where our thumbs hurt. These platforms are engineered to keep you hooked with a constant flow of notifications, updates, and personalized content. This constant stimulation can be mentally exhausting and distract you from your goals.

To that end, we recommend periodically "fasting" from social media. Delete all the social apps from your phone for a week or two to reset those unhealthy habits. If possible, schedule your social media updates so you can even take a break on your laptop as well. (We recommend services like IFTTT (If This, Then That) or Zapier to help with this.)

Set boundaries on your time
But this isn't just about deleting apps, it's about setting boundaries. Decide when and how you'll use social media. For example, you might check it for 30 minutes in the morning and again in the

evening, but not during work hours. Or, if you're an entrepreneur, you'll only use it during work hours, but not in the evening or at night.

Use tools like app timers or strategies like the Pomodoro Technique (where you set a timer for 20- or 30-minute bursts of activity) to stay within those limits. Over time, you'll find it easier to resist the urge to check your phone.

Unfollow social media influencers who actually have nothing to offer you. Sure, they're entertaining and good for a laugh, but what do they actually do for you? Instead, fill your feed with educators, mentors, and motivational figures.

Remember, you're the sum of the five people you spend the most time with. This also applies to the people you get your entertainment and information from. Be careful about who you surround yourself with on social media.

Binge-watching can be another time suck. We're not saying don't watch TV or movies. (Not at all! Some of our favorite shows are on TV!) But save it for the weekends, and limit your time during the week. Also, try to stay selective about what you do watch. Robert and Erik both love Bob's Burgers, but they limit it to one or two episodes a night.

Here's a cheat: Erik has long made it a practice to never work while he eats. That is, he doesn't believe in working through lunch or dinner, even though working from home makes this very easy. So instead, he will read or watch part of a show as he eats at his desk. (Note: He doesn't skip family meal time for this.) Rather than trying to type while not dragging his elbow through his plate, he'll watch one of his favorite shows for 20 minutes as he enjoys his lunch.

In the end, you need to be mindful of these activities and apps on your mental health. Constant exposure to social media can lead to anxiety, depression, and low self-esteem. Always being busy with extracurriculars can lead to burnout, anger, and depression.

Take steps to protect your mental well-being and limit the demands on your free time. Practice self-compassion and self-care. This will help you create more space — both time-wise and mentally — for the things that truly matter: your health, relationships, personal growth, and professional success.

Give Back to Your Community

Now that we've told you to avoid extra demands on your time, let's talk about why you should give your time and energy to others. For one thing, it can help fill emotional and spiritual needs while promoting humility, traits often linked directly with success later in life.

Giving financially reduces materialistic tendencies while donating time creates a greater sense of purpose. Community outreach isn't just good for others, it's beneficial to you as well.

Volunteering pulls you out of selfishness and reminds you that success isn't just about personal gain, it's about making a positive impact on the world around you. For some of you, that positive impact is going to happen through business. But for others, it will come through volunteering. (And for still others, that can come through both.)

Remember, success is not just about personal gain, it's about making a positive impact on the world. It's too easy to get caught up in your own ambitions and to forget about others. Volunteering provides a perspective shift and reminds you of the importance of empathy and compassion.

Volunteering can also be a great way to expand your network and build new relationships. When working alongside others who share your passion for a cause, you're likely to make meaningful connections.

These relationships can be personally fulfilling and professionally beneficial. You never know when a connection you make through volunteering might lead to a new opportunity or valuable partnership.

Volunteering can also boost your skills and knowledge. Want to learn a new skill? Volunteer at a nonprofit that will let you develop it. You could gain experience in leadership, communication, problem-solving, or event planning. Having real-world experience in any of these skills can make you a more well-rounded and marketable professional.

The idea is to find a cause that resonates with you and aligns with your values and passions. Do you care about the environment? Volunteer for a local conservation group. Are you passionate about literacy and education? Tutor children in your local area. By aligning your volunteer work with your interests, you'll be more motivated to stay involved and make a meaningful impact.

Be the CEO of Your Own Life

Robert is a big fan of Keith Ferrazzi's book, *Never Eat Alone*. In it, Ferrazzi introduces the idea of being the CEO of your own life. That means accepting responsibility for your decisions, managing your time wisely, and aligning your life's journey with a moral compass instead of depending on external circumstances or being pushed along by events outside your control.

For Robert's CEO mindset, that means prioritizing faith, family, food, fashion, and fitness. He makes sure to plan to ensure he's well-prepared for what lies ahead. It means having a strategy for the way to approach those unexpected and expected events. Like always finding time to pray, finding time to exercise, what to wear at meetings and networking events, and making sure to eat healthy.

To be the CEO of your life, start by defining your core values and understanding what you stand for. What principles will guide your decisions? Are there practices or philosophies you can study to help you understand? For Robert, it's his faith and study of the Bible; Erik has begun studying Stoicism, the ancient Greek and Roman philosophy.

Once you have a clear understanding of your values, make your career, relationships, and personal pursuits align with them. This includes the books you read, media you consume, activities you participate in, food you eat, and the people you associate with.

Next, take control of your time and energy. Time management is a critical skill for any CEO, so make sure you're spending your time on activities that move you closer to your goals and prioritizing the things that matter most.

Delegate tasks, eliminate distractions, and say no to commitments that don't align with those priorities. Turn down the opportunities that don't move you toward your goals. Even if it's just a couple of hours per month, skip those extra activities that will keep you from your path. Use to-do lists, calendars, and time-tracking apps to stay organized and focused.

Embrace Lifelong Learning and Adaptability

Regardless of your personal branding journey, or whether you even take one, the most important skill you can ever have is the ability to learn and adapt continuously. What works today might be obsolete tomorrow.

When we were graduating from college, the Internet didn't even exist, but we were both able to adapt to the new way of doing things. And as we've mastered our particular skills, new things like artificial intelligence are coming along and threatening to make us both obsolete unless we learn how to stay open to new ideas, technologies, and ways of thinking.

So, embracing lifelong learning isn't just about accumulating knowledge. It's about developing a growth mindset that allows you to thrive in a constantly changing environment. It means keeping up with what's new in the business and technology world, picking up the new skills that are necessary to grow, and putting aside the ones we no longer need.

We don't need to know how to change a typewriter ribbon or send a fax. We don't need to know how to program a VCR or make a mix tape. We don't need to know how to develop film or read a paper map. (That last one is still important, though.)

It's not that those skills aren't important; it's that technology has replaced them and made them obsolete. As the old saying goes, "There's no point in being the best buggy whip manufacturer."

The power of curiosity

You know when people create their "three words for the year" every January that will define how they pursue their goals for that year?

Number one on Erik's list is always "curiosity."

It means having a genuine desire to understand the world around you. It's what ignites that pursuit of knowledge you're going to need. It means asking questions, challenging assumptions, and seeking new experiences. It means viewing the world with a sense of wonder and being open to learning something new.

Stay curious and try to learn the cool things that a person does, or learn about some new fact or history. If you really want to stick in a person's mind when you meet them, ask them to tell you the coolest thing about their job or their industry.

Stepping outside your comfort zone

You can't learn safely inside your comfort zone. You need to try new things and take risks. It can be challenging, but it's essential for your growth. Don't be afraid to fail because that's often a valuable learning experience.

Analyze what went wrong, learn how to do it the right way, and practice over and over. Learning from your mistakes makes them a stepping stone to success.

Pursue a culture of learning

Lifelong learning is more than just an individual pursuit, it's also a cultural one. Whether you own your own business or run a department within a corporation, it's important to create a culture of learning within your organization or department.

Even if you don't run the department (yet!), it's a good habit to practice learning, as well as find other colleagues and accountability partners to learn along with you. Start a book club or a monthly lunch-and-learn practice. Encourage each other to pursue professional development opportunities and provide people with the resources necessary to learn those skills.

Make it a habit for yourself as well as your department or organization so that you can all grow together and stay more engaged. The more you all learn, the better you will all be, and the

more knowledge and value you bring to your
personal brand.

Chapter 11 Conduct Informational Interviews for Jobs and Clients

In the Mel Brooks movie, "History of the World, Part I," there's this great scene where Moses (Mel Brooks) comes down from the mountain carrying three stone tablets. He starts to speak to the Israelites and says, "I bring you these fifteen—" and then he drops a tablet — "these ten commandments!"

Since this book is *The Ten Commandments of Personal Branding*, consider this a bonus commandment.

This is an extension of Chapter 4, "The Importance of Networking." It's a strategy to help you find your next job. It can also help you if you're starting out in your new business and you need to find clients.

That, and we weren't sure if this should go into Chapter 4 or not. So we put it here; it makes it easier for people to find, since this may be one of the most important chapters of the book.

Leverage Your Network to Get Ahead in Life

Erik has a friend, Kenyon, who works in product design. He had been a product designer with the same company for 18 – 20 years, which is a long time to not be looking for a job. Most people are looking for a new job every year or two.

Even if you don't want to leave your job, it makes sense to "look" for one so you can see what the changes are in the industry and to see how you need to keep your skills fresh.

Kenyon said that because he wasn't in a job-search mindset, he wasn't prepared. No website, no portfolio, no updated résumé, nothing. So when he got laid off — which will more than likely happen to all of us at some point — he was completely unprepared. He spent the first month after he was laid off trying to build his portfolio and website so hiring managers could see the kind of work he had done.

He spent the next two or three months trying to penetrate the electronic job boards and get past the AI screeners. He got bad advice after bad advice, paid for bad service after bad service:

things like LinkedIn Premium or services that would tailor your résumé to a specific job opportunity.

Kenyon applied to at least 300 different jobs online with zero results. He got a (very) few interviews, but no job offers at all.

So he decided to try something wild and crazy: He was just going to start talking to people. He had coffee meetings with people, reached out to people he knew, and asked people for help.

(It's hard for a lot of people to admit that they're in trouble and they need help. They don't want to be seen as weak or seen as needy, and so they don't ask for help.)

Kenyon said that what happened next ended up being his favorite part of the story:

"My wife talked to one of her clients about me, and they were generous enough to say, 'I've got some people I'd like to connect you with.' And that person connected me with three or four other people. And that person connected me with [a well-known entrepreneur], and he became a mentor for me and engaged me in his business."

As a result, Kenyon launched his own business in the building permit space in 2024. He has since connected with other entrepreneurs and community leaders, and his first product will go live in Summer 2025.

He followed the same route for finding his day job as well.

The thing most people do when they lose their job is think, "A-ha! I'll reach out to my network and see what they can help me with." The problem is that if they haven't been networking professionally, the person's network is pretty much everyone they have just worked with.

And the only job those people know about is your old one.

But if you've been keeping up with your network, especially the people who left before you, those are the people you should be reaching out to.

Kenyon started reconnecting with previous coworkers online and catching up. He also said to them, "I got laid off, and I know you're working for this company. If you hear of anything, please let me know."

He started rekindling some of those old relationships, and things ebbed and flowed until one day, he got a text from one of his former co-workers who said, "Our product designer just quit. Do you want to talk to our CTO?"

The next day, he had an interview, and three weeks later, he was hired.

The moral of the story: While you can apply for all the jobs you want, the cold reality is that artificial intelligence is making it easier for people to spam jobs for ones they're not even qualified for. Which is why the HR people are fighting back with screening software that screens out nearly everyone who doesn't qualify 100% for a job.

As a result, fewer and fewer people are seen for jobs that they are ideally suited for. The HR people are receiving hundreds of applications in a matter of hours, and they're being overwhelmed by them all. The best way to get your next job is not going to be through the job boards; it's going to be through your connections.

So keep your connections fresh. Reach out to people once in a while and send them a quick text or note to let them know you're thinking about them. Meet with people who have moved on in life so they remember you exist. There may come a day when you have to ask them for a favor, and you don't want to have to remind them of who you were.

The Power of the Informational Interview

If you're looking for a job, stop looking on the job boards. Frankly, the job boards suck. Depending on who you ask, roughly 85% of jobs come through networking, although 50% of all job applications come through the job boards[9].

That means 15% of all jobs are filled through job boards. The rest comes from some sort of professional connection.

Other important job hunting statistics:
- According to HubSpot, 85% of jobs are filled through networking, not job boards.
- According to CNBC, 70% of jobs are never published publicly.

And in the days of AI-generated applications and HR screening software, these numbers are going to get worse. We know a business owner who once posted a job opening, and within a few hours, he had three hundred applications, most of whom weren't even remotely qualified for the job.

That means most jobs will get filled because you know someone, or you know someone who knows someone.

- You meet someone at a conference.

---

[9] https://www.zippia.com/advice/job-search-statistics

- A colleague tells you about an opening at their company.
- Your old boss calls you from their new company.
- A friend of a friend of a friend introduces you to a guy they know.
- You had coffee or lunch with someone in the same profession.

It's these last two that we're going to focus on. You're going to interview your way to your next job, and you're going to do it by having coffee with someone and then with someone else, and then they'll introduce you to someone else, and on and on.

Erik learned this from a friend who used this tactic in the 1980s after he moved to Indianapolis from New York. Within three months of informational interview after informational interview, he had three job offers and requests for 40 hours/week of freelance work.

This last detail is notable because most freelancers usually only hope to work 20 hours a week; the other 20 hours are spent chasing up more work.

We have both used this many times ourselves, as well as told other people about it. This advice has helped get people job interviews, internships, and brand-new jobs that they never heard about because they never showed up on any job boards.

Your job is not to find your next job.

Back in the mid-2010s, Erik was asked to speak to a job seekers support group about informational interviews. While he was there, he met a few people who had been searching for a job for months. He gave his talk and took questions from people.

One guy stood up and proudly declared that he had made job seeking his entire focus. "My job is to find my next job. I spend 8 hours a day applying to jobs." He even seemed a little smug about it.

Erik once did that in the early 2000s, and it was so disheartening. After one week of spending four hours a day on the job boards, he was so depressed, he could barely get out of bed. Erik said as much during the talk.

But the guy was undeterred. He wasn't going to let the world get him down; he was going to spend his days applying and applying and applying.

A year later, Erik was asked to come back and give the same talk again.

Guess who was still attending the same weekly meetings, using the same strategy.

Your temptation when you lose your job is to hit the job boards, nose to the grindstone, and do what our parents, our teachers, and our guidance counselors all told us we had to do, but it's all nonsense. It doesn't work that way anymore. It might have worked when you could walk into an office and drop off a résumé and come away with a job a week later.

It doesn't work like that anymore. Our world has changed so much as it is. We communicate differently, we connect differently, we consume media differently, we learn differently. So why would we find jobs the exact same way our parents and grandparents did?

If you're going to do that, why don't you just apprentice yourself out to a blacksmith or cobbler and learn a trade? Maybe you could become the best buggy whip manufacturer in the country!

Here's how to do an informational interview

Step 1: Reach out to someone in your industry, field, or company you want to work for.

Ask them if they would be willing to meet you for coffee or lunch because you want to learn more about their career and how they got there.

There is a very, very good chance that these people will want to talk to you because you have expressed an interest in them professionally, and they get a chance to talk about themselves.

If you were to call them and ask about a possible job, they almost guaranteed will not talk to you.

If you called and asked if you could do some freelance work for them, they probably won't want to talk to you.

But if you ask, "Hey, can you talk about yourself for an hour and I'll totally listen to everything you say?" they will scramble to meet you because everyone loves to talk about themselves.

Step 2: Ask them questions.

Ask them what they majored in? How did they get their first job? What do they like about it? What do they dislike?

Let them do all the talking. You can intersperse little comments like, "Oh, I hate that, too," or "I did that once." But this is not your time to do the talking, this is not your interview, it's theirs.

If they ask you questions, you can answer. But make sure they do most of the talking.

There's an old adage that the more someone else talks, the smarter *you* look. So you want to come away from this looking like a genius.

Step 3: Mute your phone!

And put it in your pocket.

Don't turn it off because you may need it to share your number or something with your interviewee. But don't keep it out where it can be a distraction.

Step 4: Take careful notes.

Get a notebook and a trusty pen. Take as many notes as you can in your notebook. Make this your interview notebook and fill it up with great advice, ideas, and stories.

Even if you never look at this notebook again, it makes you look like you're listening and paying careful attention to what the other person is saying. It's so important that you want to make sure they never forget that you did this.

Not only do they get to talk about themselves, but you think it's so valuable, you want to save it forever.

Now, you not only look like a genius, you look like a good listener.

Step 5: When it's all over, ask them two critical questions.

This is the really important part, so pay attention!

When you're nearly finished, ask the person two questions:

1. Do you know anyone else I should talk to?
2. Great, can you introduce me to them?

Because you've been such a listener, you seem really smart, and you took good notes, this person is going to be happy to recommend you to other people. You're going to ask them for a favor and they'll want to be helpful, so they'll say, "Yes, you should talk to my friend, Danielle."

And then you're going to ask them to do a mutual email introduction that connects you to Danielle.

Do **NOT** let them say, "Just tell Danielle I told you to contact her."

Because Danielle is not necessarily convinced that this person really did tell you to contact her. You could be lying. This could be a trick. Maybe you're just dropping the friend's name in the hopes that you can meet with her.

You want to avoid even the slightest appearance of that, which is why you need that email introduction.

194

Step 6: You follow up first.

Don't wait for Danielle (or whomever) to contact you first. Once you get that email introduction, follow up with the other person. Ask them the same question — "I wanted to learn more about you and your career. Can we meet for coffee?" — and then go through the same process: the listening, the note taking, the two critical questions.

Your meeting with Danielle will result in a meeting with Rosario, which will lead to a meeting with Curt, which will lead to a meeting with Javier, and so on and so on and so on.

Maybe you'll get lucky and one of them will have two introductions, and now you have two paths to follow.

But along the way, something will happen. Someone will know someone with a job opening. Or the person you talk to will be looking for someone who does what you do. Or they have a job opening at their company, and they'll put your résumé on the hiring manager's desk.

Whatever it is, you will have networked your way into a new job all without filling out a single application. You won't have visited the job boards. You'll have skipped the HR gantlet and you won't have to put up with the weeks and months of bullshit and rejections that comes with slogging it out on the job boards and classified ads like our parents and grandparents did.

GIVE informational interviews, too

One day, many years from now, you're going to be sitting at your desk and your email is going to ping (or the intracranial implant is going to buzz — we don't know what the future's going to bring), and it's going to be some 23-year-old kid who's asking *you* to sit down with them over a cup of coffee or Soylent Green or whatever we're drinking in 2048.

Take that interview. Sit down with that kid. Answer their questions and talk about yourself because this is your moment to shine and share all the cool shit you've been doing. They're going to take notes and they're not going to talk much, so they must be really smart.

And when they ask you, you're going to offer to introduce them to *two or three* of your colleagues, because you're awesome, and you're going to help this kid get started on their own career path.

Because someone did it for you, and that's how you ended up where you are.

Wrapping It Up

If you made it to the end of the book, congratulations, and thank you. This was a labor of love that was born out of a chance meeting between the two authors at a networking event organized by Chonsten Jennings, the author of the foreword of this book.

As we got to know each other over lunch and coffee meetings, we realized that while things have certainly changed since Erik's first book, *Branding Yourself* (2010), which is all about personal branding and digital marketing, the foundational principles have stayed the same.

Business is still built on relationships; opportunity still comes from knowing the right people at the right time, and that it's not just what you know or who you know, it's all about what people think about you.

You can influence what people think about you because it all starts with your actions and how you live your (public) life. If you work to help people and treat them with respect, they're going to remember you.

But if you treat them like a transaction and someone who owes you favors just because you did a favor for them, they're definitely going to remember you, they just won't think highly of you.

We've thrown a lot of information your way, but don't try to do everything at the same time or all at once. Pick one strategy or tactic from the book and start practicing it.

- Attend one networking event a month and try to meet two people.
- Send one "thinking of you" text or email to someone you haven't spoken with each week.
- Attend a local meeting of your industry's professional association.
- Write a blog article about something in your industry.
- Beef up your LinkedIn profile and start connecting with people in your industry.
- Have an informational interview with someone, even if you're not looking for a job.

Start slowly and develop a habit of some of these tactics, and pretty soon, you'll boost your personal brand and people will recognize you for the amazing work you do. Just remember to tell them where you learned how to do all this.

We have a lot of books to sell!